Platoon Sergeant's Diaries

Book 2
Operation Desert Storm
Persian Gulf War 1990-1991

236th Medical Company

Author: SFC Dewey Charles Taylor
Retired U.S. Army

Copyright © 2019
BY
DEWEY C. TAYLOR
All right reserved except for use in reviews. No part of this book is allowed to be copied, reproduced, mechanical, electronic, graphics, stored, photocopying, typing, recorded, and transmitted in any form without the author's written authorization.

Table of Contents

Table of Contents	3
Dedication	5
Acknowledgments	6
Author's Notes	9
Author's Biography	13
Introduction – Operation Desert Storm	**23**
Book 2, Diary 2 Operation Desert Storm	**24**
Day 45 Start of Operation Desert Storm	25
Day 46 Red Dragon Alert	32
Day 47 Aircraft # 579 crash	41
Day 48 Visit crew at 12th Evac Hospital	49
Day 49 Company received first female aviator	64
Day 50 Memorial Services for our Falling Comrade	67
Day 51 Six shower stalls install	70
Day 52 Platoon bike returned to Supply	74
Day 53 First flight squad received their new squad leader	79
Day 54 Staff Meeting time change by the commander	84
Day 55 Battle crews	87
Day 56 Blanket on helicopters windshield	90
Day 57 Commander talked about, "Sex in the field."	97
Day 58 Intelligent Reports-	100
Day 59 Two old fashion washing machines-	106
Day 60 Flight medics received IV training	111
Day 61 Sports day	115
Day 62 Our crew chiefs not allowed to Red X an unsafe AC	121
Day 63 Commander said he is going to start firing Soldiers	128
Day 64 Operation Security	132
Day 65 General upset about his bulldozer	134
Day 66 Phone run	137
Day 67 Latrines got plastic cover	141
Day 68 Flew to Bahrain & later spent the night in Dhahran	145
Day 69 Our crew spent another night at the 45th Med Co	151
Day 70 Flight medics had issues with new endurance sheets	159
Day 71 Vehicles got washed to prepare for their marking	163
Day 72 Training on Inflight patient form	169
Day 73 Three Iraqi Scud missiles are in air en route	172
Day 74 Anthrax Vaccine	179
Day 75 Flew to LBE to pick up a SSG from emergency leave	184
Day 76 Acting First Sergeant	187
Day 77 Medevac mission with no Flight Medic aboard	190
Day 78 Commander's Coin presented to a SGT in formation	193
Day 79 Crew and I flew to a few combat hospitals	195

Day 80	We received a new flight medic	196
Day 81	Go by the duty roster or go by assigned helicopters?	201
Day 82	I told the flight medics they have a voice	203

Southwest Asia Honor Roll --- 207
SFC Taylor returning after one of several staff meeting --- 208
236th Med Company wall plaque & photo of Czechoslovakia --- 209
Flight Platoon Sergeant & Platoon Leader met up years later --- 210
Ella & Dewey Wedding Picture --- 211
In loving Memories of my Mother --- 212
Honoring my Grandfather Service in U.S. Army during WW1 --- 213
Honoring my Brother for his service during the Vietnam Era --- 214
Final Note from Author --- 215
Military Times Conversion Chart --- 216
Rank Structure --- 217
Abbreviations – Acronyms & Definition --- 218

Dedication

This book dedicated to the One and only Living God and his Son, Jesus Christ. Also, to the brave Men and Women of the 236th Medical Company and those attached to our unit.

Staff Sergeant (SSG/E-6) Schaberg of the 236th Medical Company designed this patch for our Company.

Acknowledgments

I like to thank the 236th Medical Company members and those attached to our unit. Some we have kept in contact with over the years, and others become friends again on Facebook. Also, I want to thank the rest of the brave men and women who have served in Operation Desert Shield, Operation Desert Storm, including past and present conflicts or wars. They are real heroes for defending our great country.

Each Service Member you see should receive a thank you for their service and "Welcome Home." Sadly, the Vietnam conflict heroes did not receive the much-deserved "Thank you and Welcome Home" they so rightfully deserved. Please let us not forget them.

I like to thank Jim Mullen for some of his courtesy photos. During his tour of duty in this book, he was a Staff Sergeant and later was promoted to Sergeant First Class before he retired from the U.S. Army. We have kept in close contact over the years. I also like to thank Bob Belts, Eric Schaberg, Bob Klase, Jeff Mankoff, Penny Renee Winn, Todd

Maberry, Boyce Bingham, Bob King, Brian Lineman, John Hasselius, Gerry Wooton, Chad Holm, Steve Babine, Crispin Perez, and Brian Williams for their courtesy photos. In addition, thank you, Robyn Campbell, for your husband Don Campbell's courtesy photos.

I want to thank my previous wife, Cindy, for her support during the war, including my children, Penny, Joy, and Jonathan, who waited for me to return home.

I like to thank my present wife, Ella, who supported me in writing this book.

A big thank you to my sweet 99 years old mother, Margaret Hope Hayes Taylor, for reviewing and proofreading my book. Also, I thank my mother for supporting me during Operation Desert Shield, Operation Desert Storm, and the Vietnam War. She had to go through seeing her son go to war twice. God Bless her. Sadly, Mom passed away on 2 May 2020 at the age of 99 years old.

A thank you to my father - Dewey Clarence Taylor, who was released from the VA Hospital when I returned home from

Vietnam in 1972. The doctor said, "You're the best medicine for him." He had served in the U.S. Army during the 2nd World War and had much respect for the military. Dad passed away on 6 Nov 1979.

Also, thank you goes to my sister, Bunny Ruth Taylor Howard, for her suggestion in my books. She has always been there for me, and I am grateful to have her as my sister.

Next, I thank my brother, Tommy Nathan Taylor, who served our great country in the U.S. Army during the Vietnam era and passed away on 7 Mar 2016.

In addition, I like to thank my cousin, Leta Dale Leggett Turner, for her help in editing my book.

And I thank my cousin Delores Leggett Walker for her insight into my books, from her experience as an author of the Promise Series.

Finally, a thank you to my relatives, friends, and penpals, who kept in contact with me.

Author's Notes

To help the reader identify with the author's two diaries, the author has added a U.S. Army Rank Structure page. Also, the author has added an Abbreviations - Acronyms & Definition pages.

"Soldier" is capitalized to show honor and respect for our military personnel. Rank is spelled out with their Last name for male or First and Last name for a female to help clarify rank structure on a Soldier in this book. The only exception is when their Last name for male or female is the same.

Most of the names in this book are real. Some of them are changed per their request or to protect their identity.

The author has added information for each Day to help the reader understand, such as Day 43: 15 Jan 1991 / Tuesday. The same as in my diaries. Meaning this is the 43rd Day since we deployed with the actual date added.

Please understand, the pictures in this book are not of the best quality. Some were taken with a 110 pocket camera and later an inexpensive 35mm camera.

"I" referred to myself, Sergeant First Class (SFC/E-7) Dewey Charles Taylor, Platoon Sergeant, Senior Flight Medic, and author of this book.

In my book, the helicopter is called an Aircraft, AC, or bird and vice versa.

The characters in this book are real. Some Soldiers may have been promoted to the next higher grade while serving in Operation Desert Shield and Operation Desert Storm. The information in this book is accurate to the best of my knowledge and beliefs.

In times of war or pending conflict, people say and do things they usually would not do. We are all family, during the good or the bad times. The information stated in this book are real, but please take it with a grain of salt. Also, please don't take offense to anything in this book. I have no ill-feeling toward anyone in this book and wish nothing but their happiness throughout their life. I am very proud of the many Soldiers' accomplishments while in the military and those who choose a new civilian career path. The Soldiers I served with will always be my Brothers & Sisters in Arms, and we will always have this bond.

My story is from two diaries that I rewrote over 30 years ago. In keeping it as real as written, under combat conditions, editing for grammar was not performed to keep it realistic as possible, other than using an online program called "Grammarly Premium." In the updates, the author has gone through an edit and added additional pictures.

A special thanks to all who sent letters to Any Service Member. They may not have agreed with the war, but they show their support for us.

I like to thank all our veterans who have served and the men and women in uniform now serving. We appreciate everything they do to keep the United States of America free and safe. God Bless America, One Nation Under God.

Platoon Sergeant's Diaries

Author: SFC Dewey Charles Taylor
Retired U.S. Army

Author's Biography

Now my biography begins: I was born in Jacksonville, Florida, in 1950. I was a Boy Scout in my youth and earned my Eagle Scout Badge in 1967. I graduated from Ribault Senior High School in 1970.

I entered the U.S. Army, March 1971 and went to Basic Combat Training at Ft. Jackson, South Carolina. Upon graduation, I was promoted to Private Second Class (PV2/E-2) and received a National Defense Medal, Basic Rifle Marksmanship Badge, and Expert Grenade Badge for a starter.

I attended Advanced Individual Training (AIT) at Ft. Rucker, Alabama. I completed the OH-58 Helicopter Repair Course MOS (Military Occupation Specialist) 67V2T. Upon graduation, I got promoted to Private First Class (PFC/E-3).

At the age of 21, my first tour of duty was in Vietnam with "A Troop 7/17th Air Cavalry." There I was cross-trained on the OH-6 and UH-1 helicopter. I was a Crew Chief and Door Gunner on both. I was awarded 8 Air Medals for my Vietnam service, Crew Member Wing, Presidential Unit Citation, Cross and Gallantry with Palm, Vietnam Campaign Medal, and Vietnam Service Medal.

When we left Vietnam, our company PCS to Ft. Bragg, North Carolina. Our unit name changed to D Troop 1st Squadron 17th Cavalry. At Ft. Bragg, NC, I was a Crew Chief on UH-1 helicopter, and later OH-58 helicopter. I got promoted to Specialist 4 (SP4/E-4), received a Good Conduct Medal and Sharpshooter M-16 Badge. The training I received at Ft. Bragg was Law Enforcement at Johnston Technical Institute and Red Cross Life Saving Course. During Project Transition, I took a Radio & Television Repairman Course.

I received a Certificate of Appreciation from President Richard Nixon, our Commander in Chief. Also, I received an Honorable Discharge Certificate. After three years in service, in March 1974, I ETS (Enlisted Time Served) and went back home to Jacksonville, FL, as a civilian.

I joined the Army National Guard, located at Craig Airport, in Jacksonville, FL, Feb 1976. I went in as a Crew Chief on OH-58 helicopters. I kept the same rank I left active service with as a Specialist 4. I participated in monthly drills and went to two weeks of summer training at Camp Blanding. I joined, trying to get a full-time Civil Service position with the Army National Guard, but after six months of waiting, I decided to go back on active duty.

I contacted an Army Recruiter to see if they were allowing prior service back in. He informed me, "Because you have been out for a while, you would NOT come in with the rank of Specialist 4 (SP4/E-4) you left with; you would come in as a Private First Class (PFC/E-3). If you do not come in within the next two weeks, you will come in as a Private Second Class (PV2/E-2)."

August 1974, I enlisted and went on active duty in the U.S. Army as a Private First Class. I drove from Jacksonville, FL, to Ft. Sam Houston, Texas, for AIT to be a Medical Specialist 91B (Medic). We had a Class A Uniform inspection during a Company Formation. The Commander was inspecting the troop, and when he got to me, he was impressed; to see a PFC with so many medals and a combat patch on my right sleeve. After completing the Medical Specialist Course, I got promoted to Specialist 4.

I later PCS to the HHC 2nd Battalion, 68th Armor Regiment in Baumholder, Germany. I got selected to go to the Berlin Orientation Tours and was able to visit East Germany. I also took an EMT, Emergency Medical Technician course at the 56th General Hospital in Baumholder, Germany. I tested and became a National Register Emergency Medical Technician. I also had a military driver's license and drove the Army Gamma Goat. When we were not in the field, we worked at the Aid Station. The Soldiers would come in on the sick call, and we would treat them. I worked closely with the PA, Physician Assistant we had, and I learned a great deal.

Later, I transferred to HHC 1st Battalion, 87TH Infantry Regiment, in Baumholder, Germany. I completed the 1977 USAREUR Race Relations Orientation Program. On several occasions, I went TDY at the 56th General Hospital, Baumholder, Germany, working as an Ambulance Attendant and treating patients in the Emergency Room. In the field, I drove the APC, Armored Personnel Carrier that was also amphibious.

I have experience taking it into a deep lake and swimming it, as we called it, to the other side.

I got promoted to Specialist 5 (SP5/E-5), where I was in the HHC 1/87th Infantry. I completed the "Operating Room Specialist Correspondence Course, MOS 91D." Before I left Germany, I went to the Staff Sergeant (SSG/E-6) Promotion Board. I came real close to acing it, but would have if I knew the answer to the last question: "Where was the President's location at that time?" They did not expect a medic to do that well in an infantry outfit. Before my PCS, I received my 2nd Good Conduct Medal and Professional Development Medal.

I left Baumholder, Germany, after three years. I had orders to report to Ft. Riley, Kansas. During that time, I received a phone call that my father had passed away, so they changed my orders to leave immediately for home.

Now that it was my time to leave, there was no Commercial Airliner available, so I had to fly back to the states in a freezing C-141 Transport Aircraft. There was a casket with human remains across from where I was sitting. We landed in Dover, Delaware, where I was finally able to catch a Commercial Airliner to Jacksonville, FL.

After my father's funeral, I drove to Ft. Stewart, Georgia, and went into the 3d Platoon, 498th Medical Company. A Medevac Unit with medical UH-1 helicopters. I talked to the Commander about my experience as a National Register Emergency Medical

Technician, Medic, and Crew Chief on the UH-1 helicopter. They contacted Personnel to have my orders changed to their company. While stationed with this unit, I was a flight medic and Training NCO. Later I was promoted to Staff Sergeant (SSG/E-6) and became the Senior Fight Medic.

I applied and got accepted to the Air Traffic Control Ground Control Course (93J MOS) at Ft. Rucker, Alabama. After graduating from the Air Traffic Control Course, I PCS to USACC, Ft. Hood, Texas. At Gray Army Airfield, I was in the Control Tower as an Air Traffic Controller and shift supervisor in charge of Hood Flight Following. During the Air Traffic Control walkout (under the Reagan Administration), I re-enlisted for Ft. Carson, Colorado.

I PCS to 3rd Platoon 57th ATC Company, Ft. Carson, CO. I worked in Flight Following and Ground Approach in a tactical unit. Since I was a medic, I taught all the medical training for our company. I was one of the few selected to attend "Brim Frost 83" in Alaska from January to February 1981 for 30 days in temperature below 50 degrees zero Fahrenheit. I also participated in "Joint Readiness Exercise Bold Eagle 84" at Eglin Air Force Base, Florida.

I got promoted to Sergeant First Class (SFC/E-7). I was selected to go to an Army Reserved Company in Wyoming to train them and set up their Tactical ATC Radar equipment. I received my 3rd Good Conduct Medal and the Army Achievement Medal. The schools I attended are as follow; Airlift Planer Course, Motorcycle Improvement Course, Rail Load Planner

Course, Transportation of Hazardous Materials Course, and Mountaineering Training Course.

In February 1985, I left Ft. Carson, Colorado, and PCS to 191st ATC Company, Korea. I was the Facility Chief at Warrior Control, in charge of military and civilian personnel and the whole facility not far from the DMZ (Demilitarized Zone).

While in Korea, I earned my 1st and 2nd degree Black Belt in Tac Kwan Do. I started maxing my Physical Fitness Tests. The awards I received are as follows: 4th Good Conduct Medal, Expert M-16 Badge, and Korean Defense Service Medal. The schools I completed are Prescribed Load List, Introduction to Korean Supervision Course, and Nuclear, Biological, and Chemical Schools.

After I finished my one year tour in Korea, I PCS to United State Army Aeromedical Center, Lyster Army Hospital, Fort Rucker, Alabama. During my four year tour at Lyster Army Hospital, Ft. Rucker, AL, I was in charge of the Operating Room. Later, I had the opportunity to take over the Physical Exam Clinic as their NCOIC. I was responsible for setting up a one-day Flight Physical program. I left the Physical Exam Clinic when asked to take over the Emergency Room as their NCOIC. Later, a position came available for Plan, Operation, Training, and Security. I took over the responsibility as the Company Training NCO.

While station at Fr. Rucker, Alabama, I was selected to attend the following schools: Advance (NCOES)

Non-Commission Officer Course at Ft. Sam Houston, TX.

I met all the requirements, and I applied for the SFQC (Special Forces Qualification Course). They were looking for qualified Medics to get Special Forces qualified to become Special Forces Medic 18D MOS. I was selected to attend the October 2, 1988's Special Force Orientation Training Course. I was giving a 5-week rigorous training program to complete. My current unit is required to give me time off to train and be in top physical condition upon my arrival at Ft. Bragg, NC.

I had already completed the 5th week and was already into my 8th week of training. I was in the best physical condition ever in my whole life. While I was training, I started second-guessing myself, asking myself, is this really what you want to do? The sad part was, I talked myself out of going. August 11, 1988, I sent a letter of termination special forces training. I told them I was grateful for the selection. I know not everyone has that opportunity, and for the time, I was allowed to train.

After all that training, I was in top physical condition, so I took the Master Fitness Training Course and later completed the Air Assault Course. The other courses I took are as follows: Unit Armor Course, Basic Electronic Correspondence Course, Computer Courses, First Sergeant Course, and Instructor Training Course. The awards I received are Expert 9mm Pistol Badge, Certificate for Maximum Army Physical Fitness Tests, 5th Good Conduct Medal, Army

Commendation Medal, and "H" identifier as instructor qualified.

While station at Ft. Rucker, AL, I earned my 3rd degree Master Mason in Ozark, AL, and the 32nd degree in Scottish Rite of Freemasonry in Dothan, AL.

Later I PCS from Ft. Rucker, AL, to the 236th Medical Company in Landstuhl, Germany. I was the Platoon Sergeant with the Second Flight Platoon in charge of flight medics and crew chiefs on UH-60 Blackhawk Medevac Helicopters. In Landstuhl, I took Head Start (40 hours Gateway to Germany course). Also, I retook the EMT, Emergency Medical Technician course to brush up on my medical skills, and got certification as a National Register Emergency Medical Technician.

We received our orders for the 236th Medical Company to deploy to Saudi Arabia for Operation Desert Shield. I begin my first diary the day we left for Operation Desert Shield. I started my second diary when Operation Desert Storm war began - until all our company returned to Germany.

I received the following awards: another Air Medal, making my 9th Air Medals, Army Commendation Medal with Oak Leaf Custer, 2nd National Defense Medal, Southwest Asia Medal with bronze service stars, and Kuwait Liberation Medal - Saudi Arabia.

After we returned from Southwest Asia, I was one of two flight medics that provided medical coverage for then Vise President Dan Quayle's visit to Prague, Czechoslovakia, in June 1991. I got to meet

Ambassador Shirley Temper Black. She allowed me to take her picture and get her autograph.

Later, when asked, I became the First Sergeant of the 540th General Dispensary in Kaiserslautern, Germany. The 540th General Dispensary later moved to Landstuhl, Germany, and we share space in the 2nd General Hospital. Schools I attended while at the 540th General Dispensary are as follow: Introduction to Civilian Personnel Management for Local National Personnel, Introduction to Civilian Personnel Management for U.S. Employees, and Certificate of Training Sexual Harassment. Also, I joined the European Shrine Club in 1992.

Before I PCS'd from Germany, I had orders to the Joint Readiness Training Center in Arkansas. Later, those orders changed to a Command in Ft. Belvoir, Virginia. Once I reported there, I found out my order has changed to the Joint Readiness Training Center at Ft. Poke, Louisiana.

While on leave in the states, I bought an Army Time Newspaper. I am number seven on the Master Sergeant Promotion List for E-8 for my MOS 91B. So I called DA, Department of the Army, and was informed my order has already changed to Ft. Bragg, North Carolina.

I PCS'd to the 56th Medical Battalion, Ft. Bragg, North Carolina, as the Operation Sergeant. I completed my last year in the Army there.

Once I put in my paperwork to retired, I was able to work at the Ft. Bragg Music Center during the night and attend Truck Driving Training classes on base during the day. While working at the Music Center, I met and shook hands with Gary Burghoff (Radar O'Reilly) from the MASH TV show.

In August 1993, I retired with 20 Honorable plus years of military service in the U.S. Army, and I received the Meritorious Service Medal and Certificate of Retirement. I also received my certification to be an ROTC Instructor for the High Schools.

Platoon Sergeant's Diaries
Introduction
Operation Desert Storm

Name given for the military operation in which international coalition forces, including British and U.S. lead troops, were sent to protect Saudi Arabia after Iraq invaded Kuwait and removed Iraqi dictator Saddam Hussein's army from Kuwait.

A true story from my diaries as a Platoon Sergeant, Senior Flight Medic, station at 236th Medical Company, in Landstuhl, Germany, while deployed to the Persian Gulf. This book is a series of my two diaries serving in Operation Desert Shield and Operation Desert Storm.

"Platoon Sergeant's Diaries, Diary 1 - Operation Desert Shield," Book 1, is from 4 Dec 1990 to 16 Jan 1991. Starting from Day 1, the Departure from Landstuhl, Germany, where the stories begin to Day 44, the last day of Operation Desert Shield in Saudi Arabia.

"Platoon Sergeant's Diaries, Diary 2 – Operation Desert Storm," Book 2, is from 17 Jan 1991. It starts with Day 45 at the beginning of Operation Desert Storm, where Book 1 left off to Day 82. Book 3 start Day 83, the day the Ground War began, and continues to Day 128. Finally, book 4 starts on Day 129, with the question about the Humanitarian Efforts in Turkey, though Day 155/Day 204, after returning to our U.S. base in Germany.

This book is the Combat History of the 236th Medical Company and those attached to our unit. It gives accounts for each day. It is a true story, and I am honor to have served with these great Soldiers. They will always be family and my Brothers and Sisters in Arms.

Book 2
Platoon Sergeant's Diaries
Diary 2

Operation Desert Storm

Day 45: 17 Jan 1991 / Thursday - Start of Operation Desert Storm

At approximately 0330 hours (3:30 am) this morning, we were woke up and told to go to MOPP Level 2 (put on our Protective Overgarment, Overboots, carry our Protective Mask with hood and gloves) and go to the bunkers. The first initial war has started.

Major Becker, our Commander, stopped by our bunker and asked, "Is the 236th Medical Company here?" We said, "Yes, Sir." Then he gave us an update and asked if we have any questions? I asked, "What about the chemical pills, PB Tablets (Pyridostigmine Bromide – Anti-nerve agent pill, pretreatment against nerve agent soman)? He said, "You may take it now." Someone asked him, "Have you taken yours yet?" Our Commander said, "I have not taken one yet." After that, one officer said, "I'll take mine after you take yours." I was thinking; I don't know what side effects this medication may have. If it gave me diarrhea and being cram-packed in this bunker, I may not get out in time. Therefore, I did not take one either.

Later, one of the Soldiers went by each bunker and threw in a couple of boxes of M9 Papers (chemical detector paper, used to identify the presence of liquid chemical agent aerosols, nerve, and mustard agents), and told us to put a strip on our left arm and one piece on the right leg. (The paper will turn pink, red, reddish-brown, or red-purple when exposed to a liquid agent.)

Meanwhile, Mr. (W01) Gambrel and Mr. (CW2) Clark listened to their radio in the bunker. They kept us informed of what was going on. They said, "The U.S. Air Force, Saudi, Britain, Kuwait, Egyptians bomb Baghdad and Kuwait. Over 400 bombings took place, taking out the chemical, nuclear, and artillery capability." Later they said, "All the planes were returning. The mission was a success." Our Commander stopped by the bunkers when he heard the good news. He said, "Next time I go to the Ramstein, Germany, Air Force Officer's Club, I will buy them all a round of drinks."

We listen to President George W. Bush Sr. broadcast over the radio while we were in the bunker.

Next, President George W. Bush Senior broadcast over the radio and gave the reason for the attack. He said, "We could not wait no longer. We had the perfect window of opportunity, and I gave the order."

We could see the jets as they flew back south. At about 0700 hours (7 am), the First Sergeant said, "We are on our second attack with Iraq. We stayed in the bunker until about 0730 hours (7:30 am).

Then I went back into the tent and fixed myself a cup of Mocha. CPT Swingle came into the tent to give us an update. While we were still in our tent, CPT Connell came up to me and asked to get four flight medics to pull perimeter guard for about one hour, so the 818th Medical Brigade guards could get something to eat. I got SSG Sims, SSG Miller, SSG Lucia Gabriela, SSG Denzel, SSG Niles, and Mr. (WO1) McKenny.

CPT Babine walked back in; I informed him what was going on. He said, "CPT Dodson did not want the Crew Chief to pull any of the guard duty and that he was going to the Commander. SPC Lineman (Crew Chief) said, "I will help pull guard duty." I informed the First Sergeant for the 818th Medical Brigade, "Do not pay any mind to CPT Dodson." Then I walked out with the Soldiers that were pulling guard duty around the perimeter.

I came back to the tent and fixed myself another cup of Mocha. I heard they did a job on the Iraq communication and wiped out their air forces. It is now 0915 hours (9:15

am). The attack took off at 1900 hours (7 pm) Eastern Standard Time. All the aircraft flew low at 50 feet, not to be detected, pop up 200 feet, drop their bombs, and leave. They now called this war "Operation Desert Storm."

Operation Desert Storm started today.

We had our Staff Meeting tonight at 1800 hour (6 pm). Our Commander said, "We will be going back to our airfield at AL Qaisumah tomorrow morning. Our mission most likely will be flying west of the Neutral Zone, the border, and back to the 12th Evac Hospital." He informed us, "50 tanks of the Iraq army gave up. The fleeing Iraqi soldiers need to report to me. We most likely will get a flock of reporters, and if we do, they will need to see me."

Then our Commander said, "The U.S. Army, Apache Attack Helicopter (AH-64) was on the initial attacks in Kuwait on the Iraqi tanks. Twenty-three aircraft from Iraq was headed south this morning and was intercept by our guys and was either shot down or made to turn back. I heard an A-10 Thunderbolt Bomber blowing up tanks right and left. Iraqi launched three Scud missiles; two got shot down, one that misfired and missed its target. One of the Scud missiles that got shot down was going to Israel."

Next, our Commander informed us, "We are presently at MOPP Level 1 (wearing our Overgarment, and carrying our Protective Mask with hood, Overboots & Gloves). But need to be ready to get into MOPP Level 2 (wearing our Overgarment, Overboots, and carrying Protective Mask with hood & Gloves) and go back into the bunker."

Our Commander continues by saying, "The Iraqi still have mobile Scud missiles and biological weapons capability." Then our Commander said, "The old bunkers had been rebuilt today, made new, improved, and located right outside the tents. You need to know where the bunkers are." Next, he said, "You need to know which helicopter or vehicle to go on in case we activate our Scatter Plan (Evacuation Plan). Presently aircraft # 676 won't fly, so we will not count on that helicopter."

Our Commander also said, "I want SGT Red to get more nerve agent antidotes for our troops and check on getting more medical supplies, such as MES equipment (Medical Equipment Sets) to replace the two helicopters that do not have them." I also spoke up and said, "We need to check on getting Morphine Sulfate (M.S.) for treating Soldiers for pain."

Before we left, CPT Babine wanted to talk to everyone who used to live in the Supply tent. I don't recall the reason. After the meeting, I checked the location of those four bunkers in case needed.

This evening, I was covering for SSG Crispin Perez flight medic duty for night 1st Up. Later, SSG Crispin Perez informed me, "I will go ahead and pull night 1st Up duty on my aircraft." He said, "I still have SSG Miller MES equipment (Medical Equipment Sets, litters/transport bed, oxygen with stand attachment, and IV poles) on my helicopter."

Also, tonight, I had to pick two flight medics to pull guard duty here at the 818th Medical Brigade. I choose SGT Red for 0200-0400 hours (2 am – 4 am) and SSG Miller 0400-0600 hours (4 am – 6 am).

This evening I received some mail. I received three letters from Cindy for 22, 23, and 24 Dec 1990. I was glad to hear from home. It is getting late, and I am getting tired. I only ate an MRE for lunch, and then I ate a small portion of it. It is now 2206 hours (10:06 pm), and we are still at MOPP Level 1. I hope we get a good night's sleep tonight without us getting under attack.

Day 46: 18 Jan 1991 / Friday

I woke up this morning at 0500 hours (5 am). I got up and went to the restroom. Good time to go before the flies wake up. It gets crowded and hot. While I was there, I heard Soldiers yelling, "Go into the bunker, 'Red Dragon.'"(A code word, meaning to go into the fallout shelters, a possible Iraq Scud missile has been launch.) Therefore, I went into the bunker. I notice they better construct than yesterday and much more in-depth.

When we got the "All Clear," SGT Walling, SGT Denman, and I went to breakfast. There we picked up two MREs and a juice. We walk back into the 818th Medical Brigade area. The First Sergeant for the 818th Medical Brigade said, "Thank you, SFC Taylor, for providing me two guards for last night guard duty."

We had Company Formation at 0800 hours (8 am). I had just enough time to brush my teeth but not enough time to shave. At formation, our Commander was concerned about a missing set of Night Vision Goggles (NVG). The Commander ordered us to go out to each helicopter and search for those missing NVG. We searched all the helicopters without coming up with the Night Vision Goggles. Later, Mr. (WO1) McKenny said, "I found the missing NVG in the 818 Medical Brigade Supply tent. It must have fallen behind their supply or were hiding there."

After that, CPT Babine identified the crew that will be staying at the 818 Medical Brigades. Our company took down the two G.P. medium tents and loaded them on the 2 ½ ton truck. The rest of us packed our gears and laid them outside of our tents.

I told SSG Lucia Gabriela, "You need to go back to the company and bring your bags and stay. Also, I want you to get SSG Crispin Perez bags together at the company. I make sure I get his bags back to him. While at the company, I want you to get the medical aid bags together." SSG Lucia Gabriela said, "I want to stay here for my training. If I go back to the company, I will end up doing detail and not getting the training I need."

She looks like she was fixing to cry. I told her, "I will get with CPT Babine, and if he agrees, you can stay here at the 818th Medical Brigade and train with SSG Crispin Perez since they decided to keep the crew tent here." Later I saw CPT Babine, and I informed him of the situation, and he said, "It is okay with me."

The next thing I knew, as I was walking out of the tent, I saw SSG Belt and SSG Lucia

Gabriela driving off in the 2 ½ ton truck. I immediately waved for them to stop. They came back, and I got SSG Mullen to help load our bags on the 2 ½ ton truck. SSG Lucia Gabriela informed me, "I have a ride back to the 818th Medical Brigade in a helicopter." SSG Clark and a few of us climbed into the truck's back, and we headed back to the company.

As soon as we got back to the unit, we had Company Formation. The only ones in my platoon present were SSG Miller, SSG Sims, and SGT Homer. After the formation, the drivers did PMCS on their vehicles. The rest of the company helped put up the G.P. medium tent. SSG Miller took care of the NVG for the Commander. SGT Homer and I worked on straightening up our tent. I help sweep out the tent and straighten out my area. SGT Homer was displeased with his space. I informed him, "If you like, I will trade with you."

Later, SSG Miller got on my case about his MES equipment being aboard, SSG Crispin Perez helicopter. Then SGT Homer and SSG Sims also got in on the subject. By that time, CPT Babine stops by the tent. He said, "This is an NCO matter. I am aware of the problems." I told SGT Homer, "You have a choice to either loan SSG Miller your MES equipment or pull his First-up duty."

A little while later, SSG Crispin Perez returned. I told him, "I need SSG Miller MES Equipment off your helicopter to give back to SSG Miller. SSG Crispin Perez said, "No problem." I informed him, "Since you have two Aid Bags, a long backboard, and a short backboard, you can still stabilize the patients. Presently you do not have a hand receipt for any MES equipment, and SSG Miller does. Also, I am working on getting more equipment." I suggested SSG Crispin Perez, "You could check with the 12th Evac Hospital. Maybe you could sign for a set from them."

Later, we got all the personal belonging for those flight medics staying at the 818th Medical Brigade and put those bags on SSG Crispin Perez bird that is returning there.

At about 1400 hours (2 pm), we had a hot lunch. It was good too. The Dinner Facility Mess Sergeant, SFC Mason, told me, "Since you are a Platoon Sergeant, come back later. I have something for you."

After I ate, I went back to see him. He gave me a big box of P.X. items, such as soaps, foot powders, and other things. I went back and divided it between my two flight squads. By then, it was time for the 1800 hours (6 pm) Staff Meeting. So I left to attend the meeting.

At the meeting, our Commander said, "Expects B-52 Bombing strikes follow by armor tanks going north to be happening soon. Also, our fence perimeters now have claymore mines and for us not to walk past the helicopters." He also informed us, "A Soldier yesterday accidentally shot his right shoulder with his M16 rifle. He had it locked and loaded (meaning it had a round of ammo in the chamber). Weapons are not to be locked and loaded."

Our First Sergeant said, "SSG Clint and SFC Inniss will drive M-2 Blazer vehicle on the Scatter Plan now. Then our Commander said, "I want classes for the crew chiefs for two hours on accidents and NVG.

Our Commander said, "Do not take the P.B. tablets for chemical, as it has side effects. A few Soldiers told me they had stomach cramps, dry mouth, and made their nose drain." The Commander also said, "If the P.B. tablets are taken together along with the Malaria pill, it can cause convulsion."

Our First Sergeant said, "Tomorrow, I want flight medics for detail duties. Since the flight medics are in the area and can still be available for their mission, the other platoons will have other duties. Tomorrow's detailed assignment is SSG Sims, SGT Homer, SGT Red, and SGT Gold." Then our First Sergeant said, "SFC Taylor, I want a tent diagram for both flight squads." So I provided him with a tent diagram for both flight squads.

Our Commander said, "After 2030 hours (8:30 pm), all driving off the airfield will be in blackout condition, including all helicopters taking off and departing the airfield. In the morning, at 0500 hours (5 am), we will be in 'Stand-To,' in MOPP Level 1."

Then our Commander said, "Civilian clothes are only authorized to the shower from your tents. You must wear a minimum of your helmet, weapon, and protective mask—also only one bath every other day to conserve water. The Scatter Plan location is the 818th Medical Brigade. We need to anticipate evacuating the airfield again. There will be duel pilots that will take off and return to pick up more Soldiers if time allows. All vehicles will leave that are operable. There will be a day and night crew at the 818th Medical Brigade and here at the DUSTOFF (Medevac name). The hospital called themselves "BANDAID."

Our Commander said, "I am assigning CPT Dodson the duty of appointing combat crews for the helicopters." He then said, "The password for tomorrow is, 'Quarter & Freedom.'" Next, our Commander said, "The plywood we have is for the shower and for no one to mess with them." Then our Commander said, "Operation tent will have green outdoor carpet put on the floors." CPT Babine asked, "What about the GAM Global Immunization?" Our Commander replied, "Everyone will take it if they had it or not."

After the meeting, CPT Babine got with me, and we talked about who is assigned to which aircraft, the TDY site, and their aircraft with crews. We also spoke about Medical Equipment Set. After that, I went and informed both flight squads of the new information. Then I passed out goodies that I had for them. Later, Mr. (CW3) Young came to get SSG Miller for a mission.

It is now about 2230 hours (10:30 pm), and I was getting ready to go for a shower. Then someone yelled out, "Red Dragon" (Iraq Scud alert). We all had to get in our bunker. Later, SSG Miller came back and got in the shelter. Also, SSG Davis and CPL Voss got in the bunker with us too. The Commander and First Sergeant checked on our status through a field phone. Our First Sergeant said, "If this turns out to be a chemical, we will go into our tent and stay in MOPP Level 1." Our Commander informed us, "An Iraq Scud was launch, but we do not know in what direction and for us to stay in our bunker."

Later, our First Sergeant stopped by our bunkers. He informed the Second Flight Squad, "All Clear." Then he said, "We are now in MOPP Level 0. (Meaning to carry our Protective Mask with hood and have readily available our Overgarment, Overboots, and

Gloves.) You can all go back into your tent now."

It is about midnight as I am writing in my diary, goodnight.

Day 47: 19 Jan 1991 / Saturday

We were woke up this morning at 0445 hours (4:45 am) and told to go to Stand-To, meaning to go to our assigned bunker and wait for further instruction on the field phone. We initially had a Stand-To schedule for 0500 hours (5 am). I heard later bunker number 3 never answered their field phone.

After the Stand-To, we went to Company Formation as instructed. At formation, the Commander clarified what to do when we get, "Stand-To or Red Dragon." He said, "We are to go into our bunker and wait for further instruction. If we get hit with a chemical weapon, we will go into MOPP Level 4 and go into our tent when order. The reason for this, the chemical will settle down to the lowest places."

The Commander continues to say, "If we get a "Red Dragon Alert," we are to go into

MOPP Level 1, and if you have a mission, you will go like that."

After Company Formation, we had a police call (picking up trash). After that, SSG Miller went and got fuel for our heater. Today we got issued our 2nd Ice Pack. I attached mine to the back of my rucksack to be ready if I should need it.

Later, I made up a "Status Board," with all the Aircraft numbers, their assigned Flight Medic, Crew Chief, and Pilot in Charge, Co-Pilot, and Remark. Also, a place to checkmarks for the Scatter Plans. The Status Board I have hanging on the wall of my tent next to my cot. Now I can tell at a glance where my flight medics are, which aircraft is who, remarks of any flight medics location changes, such as Forward Supports, etc.

At 1130 hours (11:30 am), I washed my clothes by hand. While I was cleaning them, my back started hurting real bad and still giving me pain. As I washed my clothes, I saw several C-130 Aircraft (U.S. Air Force Transport Plane) fly here to this airport. There was one right after the other. Then I saw many OH-58D helicopters (Kiowa

Warrior Armed Reconnaissance Helicopter) & CH-47 Helicopters (Chinook, twin-engine, Troop movement & Supplies helicopter) flying north.

After I washed my clothes, I went to get a hot meal for lunch. It was pretty good too. I talked to the NBC NCO SFC Butch; he was upset with Operation Leaders. They would not listen to his advice or let him into the TOC (Tactical Operations Center).

My back was still hurting, so I laid on my cot and read on Nuclear, Biological, and Chemical. I also read up on the M9 Chemical Detection Paper's uses and MOPP Gear exchange (Mission-Oriented Protective Postures, Overgarment, Mask with hood, Overboots & Gloves) in my Common Tasks Manual.

At 1645 hours (4:45 pm), I took a nice, warm shower. I notice the ladies in this company sure used up a lot of water. Well anyway, when I returned to my tent, change clothes, SPC Barnes came into our tent. He told SSG Sims, "You have to get your medical gear off the aircraft, as we are keeping the crew and taking the aircraft." I overheard the conversation, and I said, "Wait a minute." The other flight medics in the tent said, "You need to take care of this." I said, "I will."

I went and talked with CPT Babine, and he did not know anything about this. He said, "You go to your tent and wait for me, and I will go to Operation." While waiting in the tent, Mr. (CW3) Hunter came by; I informed him, "The aircraft fly with their assigned flight medic and crew chief." I also told Mr. Hunter, "I have already talked with CPT Babine about this, and he said he would switch tomorrow."

Mr. Hunter told me to come with him to Operation. I informed him, "CPT Babine told me to go to my tent and wait for him." He said, "I told you to come with me, and that was your last order." Therefore, I followed him to Operation. CPT Babine and CPT Dodson both told him the same thing, "The crews stay with their assigned bird." He acted like he was in such a big hurry and said, "I have to go to my mission." CPT Babine replied, "You on a mission?" Mr. Hunter said, "Not exactly; I just want to get back to our area."

Later, I saw SSG Sims; he said, "I am getting my equipment off the aircraft." SSG Sims asked me to get a vehicle for him to move the equipment. When we got to SSG Sims aircraft, he had just about everything out of the helicopter as far as medical equipment.

The next thing I knew, I saw SSG James with my medical equipment putting it on SSG Sims bird. That would cause Aircraft # 550 not to have any medical gear. I told them to take it back to AC # 550, that it stays with the aircraft.

Then Mr. (CW3) Hunter & Mr. (CW2) Dixon got into it with me. I said, "I have signed for this med gear." They would not listen to me. So I told them, "I am going to talk with CPT Babine," and started walking away. Mr. (CW2) Dixon yelled at me and said, "SFC Taylor, Come Back, STOP," and then said, "If you take one more step, you will get an Article 15." So I decided I would stop and see what he has to say.

He got up in my face, so I got in his face too. Then he told me, "Get in a position of Attention." He yells some, and so did I. Then he told me, "Shut up and hear me out." I told him, "If the medical equipment is taking off from AC # 550, it would not be mission ready." He said, "AC # 550 is grounded (meaning not able to fly for a mechanical reason) and would be for a while."

Then Mr. (CW3) Hunter came and said, "You all should not be doing this in front of the troop." So I said, "Alright, you can use my equipment for tonight." Then he said, "We are at war, and it doesn't matter whose medical equipment is whose." I said, "It does, and I have been all through this before."

When we got back to the aircraft, SSG Sims agreed to let SSG James use his medical equipment until tomorrow. SSG Sims said, "My aircraft needed a battery." So we put my med gear back on AC # 550.

SPC Barnes was a little upset as he wanted to go with his bird, but now he is going tomorrow.

I went to the Staff Meeting. After the meeting, I talked with CPT Babine and told him the whole story. He said, "I will take care of it." I asked him, "Was I wrong?" He said,

"No." I informed him, "I should not have to enforce this policy." He said, "You are right, SFC Taylor."

While back in the tent, SSG James came in. I guess the weather was too dangerous to fly. SSG James was quite upset. On top of that, he said, "I do not have a sleeping bag." I don't know the reason for that. Maybe it is on another aircraft or another site.

Later that evening, Mr. (WO1) Gambrel came into our tent. He said AC # 579 had a crash and not to go into the Operation tent. He said, "A lot is going on." A while later, I talked with the First Sergeant. He informed me, "SSG Schaberg was hurt." I reply, "I hope he is alright." Right then, I said a silent prayer that the crew would be alright. SSG James asked about SSG Hailey. The First Sergeant did not report any more about it.

Mr. Gambrel came into our tent to inform us AC # 579 had crashed. On the right is Mr. Gambrel, and on the left-hand side of the picture is SSG Crispin Perez.

After the First Sergeant left, SSG James went to Operation. When he returned, he informed us what he found out. He said, "There were seven people aboard the aircraft. One flight medic and another patient were hurt. I am thinking to myself; this is a sad night. Please, God, allow SSG Schaberg and SSG Hailey, and the rest of the crew to be alright and not hurt.

Tonight, I got a word that the airport and town here are total blackouts (all lights turned off to prevent the enemy from seeing from the air or ground for possible targets). I sure hope nothing happens tonight.

Later, Mr. (WO1) Gambrel and CPT Babine came into our tent at about 2045 hours (8:45 pm). They were asking me if I had a record of SSG Hailey next of kin. I asked them, "Is SSG Hailey alright?" They said, "We don't know." Then said, "The person who was injured real bad the last name starts with an, "H." So they figure it would be SSG Hailey." They also woke up SSG James and asked him if he knew anything about SSG Hailey and any information about his next kin. SSG James said, "No, Sir, and all his stuff is at Log Base Alpha."

My feeling, I sure hope they are all alright. But I have a terrible feeling about SSG Hailey. He did not want to be here in the first place. He has never been a flight medic, nor did he want to be a flight medic. He always said, "I do whatever you want."

Day 48: 20 Jan 1991 / Sunday

We were woke up at 0445 hours (4:45 am) to be ready for Stand-To at 0500 hours (5 am). At about 0455 hours (4:55 am), SSG

Davis came into our tent and told us about the helicopter crash status. He said, "Flight Medic SSG Schaberg had a fractured ankle. Crew Chief SPC Garcia had a penetrating wound to his rear end. SSG Hailey, who was under Flight Medic Training, had an injury to the back of his head. He died five minutes after getting on the back of a ground ambulance."

Then SSG Davis said, "I heard SSG Hailey flight helmet must have come off. SSG Hailey was treating a patient at the time of the crash. I heard the helicopter was turning in the flight position for a landing. The helicopter tore in half, and one rotor blade is stuck straight up in the ground. The Pilots were: Mr. (CW3) Anderson and Mr. (WO1) Kreg. There were two patients aboard the helicopter." He said, "The information I received was from SPC Voss, who went with MAJ Becker (our Commander) last night.

At 0600 hours (6 am), the First Sergeant instructed us to use this time for personal hygiene, breakfast and be ready for 0730 hours (7:30 am) Company Formation. In formation, our Commander put out the information about the crash. He started getting watery eyes when he said, "SSG Hailey killed, and the others are injured."

After formation, CPT Babine wanted to talk with all the flight medics in our tent. He spoke of the accidents. It was a sorrowful time. He said, "Mr. (CW3) Anderson hurt his back; SSG Schaberg fractured his ankle, SPC Garcia had a penetration of his rear end, Mr. (WO1) Kreg was okay but admitted for evaluation."

Later, I asked the First Sergeant if I could see the crews? He said, "Not at this time because of the investigation."

Today, I found out SSG Hailey lives in the same stairwell quarter (military housing) in Germany as SGT Byrd and SSG Clark. From what I hear, "Crew rest was an issue, and no crew members are getting enough rest."

Later, CPT Babine informed me, "Mr. (CW3) Hunter crews will be one of the combat crews." CPT Dodson said, "SFC Taylor, I want you to check the aircraft to see if they have medical equipment, or at least the minimum medical gears aboard."

I tasked this with both flight squads. I had SSG Denzel in the first squad flight medic's checks their assigned aircraft and ensured everything is secured. I also had the second squad flight medics check their assigned aircraft for the same. I also physically checked all the nine helicopters that are here.

M-25 the wreck 5 Ton Truck that SSG Fox and SPC Roberson were driving.

Our First Sergeant also informed me, "M-25 (5-ton truck) had an accident; SSG Fox and Specialist Roberson are okay."

After checking all the aircraft, our First Sergeant said, "SFC Taylor, you will ride with SFC Forest. He will drop you off at the 12th

Evac Hospital, so you can have your back checked out. When you get done, go to the 818th Medical Battalion."

The crashed site of Aircraft # 579 next to the 12th Evac Hospital on Saturday night 19 Jan 1991, in Saudi Arabia.

Once we arrived in the area, it was foggy. SPC Burgoon said, "Is that the helicopter that crashed?" You could hardly see it, but it was. Just past the pilot's seats, the helicopter's front nose separated from the rest of the aircraft body.

SFC Forest drop me off at the entrance to the 12th Evac Hospital. There the guard told me, "Halt, who goes there?" Then the guard gave the challenge password. I returned to the female guard, the other part of the password. Then she asked to see my ID (Identification) card. After that, she informed me to sign in at the gate.

When I got in, I asked where sick call (military personnel requiring medical attention) located? A Soldier there pointed me in the right direction. I found where the sick call is at and saw Major Becker, our Commander. He told me where the crews are. I asked him, "Is it okay for me to go see them?" He said, "Yes." I walked into the Sick Call Emergency Treatment Area, and one of them asked me what was wrong? I told him it was my back. He directed me to the Orthopedic Clinic. So I walked in and saw Mr. (CW3) Anderson. I spoke with him for a few minutes. He said, "I am okay, except for my back."

I also saw and spoke with SPC Garcia and Mr. (WO1) Kreg. SPC Garcia said, "Something penetrated through my rear end, but I am doing alright." Mr. (WO1) Kreg shows me his flight suit where something went through and tore it. He only got minor cuts and bruises. I asked, "Where is SSG Schaberg? They said, "He is right next door."

So I walk next door and saw SSG Schaberg, and we talk for a while. I gave him a pack of candy Life Savers, some envelopes, and papers to write letters. I had some in my flight suit pant pocket that I was wearing. I noticed his left ankle was all bandaged up. He said, "I have a fractured ankle, a couple of pull ligaments, my left knee is bruised, and left elbow swollen with bruises. Also, I have some minor cuts, bruises, and abrasions."

I could tell he was depressed about SSG Hailey. He said, "SSG Hailey was doing a great job. He would have completed his entire Flight Medic Training that night." I asked, "Did SSG Hailey have his flight helmet on?" He said, "Yes, and chinstraps were button too." SSG Schaberg said, "SSG Hailey was treating the patients while they were coming in for a landing at the 12th Eval Hospital.

Bob King (Cilven Contractor) and SPC Tony Martinez at the crash site. Courtesy photo of Bob King.

This photo was taken of SSG Schaberg instructing SSG Hailey (Woody) how to adjust his flight helmet just days prior. SSG Schaberg in the center, and to his left is SSG Hailey. Photo courtesy of SSG Schaberg.

I told SSG Hailey to sit down and handed him the rear seat belt to put on. SSG Hailey was in the process of bucking his seat belt." Then SSG Schaberg said, "I got to my seat, buckled and tightened my seat belt. The next thing I remember litters (military stretchers) with the patients was going forward. I reached and grabbed the handlers with both hands as it went up. That is all I remember."

SPC Garcia said, "I unbuckled my seat belt and ran to SSG Schaberg, who was spread eagle (arms outstretched and legs apart like the letter "X") with his face in the ground. My first thought was SSG Schaberg was dead. I shook SSG Schaberg, and he came to and asked what happened?" SPC Garcia replied, "We crash." Then SPC Garcia said, "SSG Schaberg jumped up, ran to the helicopter, grab his aid bag, and found SSG Hailey. He intubated SSG Hailey, and Mr. (WO1) Kreg administers CPR (Cardiopulmonary Resuscitation) on him."

SSG Schaberg said, "SSG Hailey had a weak pulse. A doctor wanted to go ahead and pronounced him dead, but I said, 'No doctor, he is one of our.' Therefore, they worked on him longer but were not able to bring him back."

SSG Schaberg asked me, "Will you contact my wife, Karen, to let her know that I am alright? I told him, "I will." Then SSG Schaberg asked me to ask the Commander for three things:
1) Order be cut for SSG Hailey, awarding him the crew member wing.
2) SSG Schaberg to accompany SSG Hailey's body back to Germany.
3) SSG Schaberg to be allowed to stay with his crew.

After that, I went and saw the Orthopedic Doctor, MAJ Child. He examines me and then sent me off to get an x-ray. When they were ready, I return with the x-ray. The doctor looked at it and said, "I see no fractures." Then he said, "What you probably have is some overwork strained muscles." He gave me a prescription for some Motrin 600 mg. I went to the pharmacy there and picked them up.

Then I stopped back by to say goodbye to SSG Schaberg, SPC Garcia, Mr. (WO1) Kreg, and Mr. (CW3) Anderson.

Photo of Aircraft # 579 at the crashed site next to the 12th Evac Hospital in Saudi Arabia. Crashed happens Saturday night, 19 Jan 1991.

Additional helicopter crash pictures courtesy of SSG Schaberg.

More helicopter crash pictures courtesy of SSG Schaberg.

I left there and walked up to the crash helicopter site. I walked as far as the MP (Military Police) would allow me to go. The MP said, "They have been there all night." They were pretty nice. They let me walk around their vehicle 360 degrees to have a good look at the crash site. The helicopter nose was on its right side with the pilots and crews window section and main wheels separated, twisted apart from the helicopter facing the opposite direction. The parts were all over the area, rope off and with MP guards. It's a wonder anyone survived at all.

After I left there, I headed toward the 818th Medical Battalion. CPT Connell saw me and gave me a ride there. I stopped and talked with SSG Crispin Perez and SPC Thompson. They said, "SSG Mullen and SSG Lucia Gabriela took off in a bird to the area last night. The only one left there was a pilot and SPC Garcia." The pilot said, "SSG Lucia Gabriela did a good job." SSG Crispin Perez said, "I too walked to the crash site area." While we were talking, I warmed myself an MRE for lunch and took my Motrin 600 mg.

I went to S-1, the Military Personnel Office at the 818th Medical Battalion, and got a letter from Mom dated 29 Dec 1991. SGT Cauthorn wanted to see me. He asked me, "How old is SSG Hailey?" I told him, "He is 42 years old. Also, his flight record show 1953 was his date of birth."

Later, I asked SSG Lucia Gabriela and SSG Crispin Perez, and they both said SSG Hailey was 42 years old. Before I left, SSG Mullen and SSG Lucia Gabriela had to take off on a mission. Then SSG Crispin Perez had a medevac mission.

Later I saw Major Becker, our Commander. I informed him, SSG Schaberg had three requests of you:

1) Orders to be cut for SSG Hailey awarding him Crew Member Wing.
2) SSG Schaberg to escort SSG Hailey's body back to Germany.
3) SSG Schaberg to be allowed to stay with his crew.
Major Becker shucked his head up and down and said, "Okay."

The First Sergeant came and got me when it was time to go back to our site. SGT Cauthorn was in the Land Rover vehicle too. Our First Sergeant said, "The 101st Airborne Division had left and is already in Iraq. The 213th Medical Company is going west of Kuwait." He also said, "The MI (Military Intelligent) Company in moving back to our area. Several other companies are moving in too." We got back in time for a hot supper and to pick up two MREs. After I ate my hot dinner, I wrote some in my diary. Then I read Mom's letter.

After that, I went to the Staff Meeting at 1800 hours (6 pm). Our Commander said, "Tuesday at 1300 hours (1 pm) is a Memory Service for SSG Hailey." Then our Commander said, "No one can call Germany and say anything about the helicopter accident. The Casualty Assistance Officers has to do that."

CPT Babine informed me, "AC # 969, SSG Denzel bird is going TDY to LBA to pull day duty. Also, AC # 736 will be Day and Night First-up." CPT Babine asked me to pick two flight medics, one for Days First-up and one for Night First-up. For First-up Day, I decided on SSG Sims, and First-up Night, I picked SSG Miller.

When I got back to our tent, there was smoke everywhere. SSG Sims was trying to put the fire out in the heater so he could turn it off. I went to Supply and asked SSG Diane Riggins for another heater. She said, "I will try to find you one tomorrow." I informed her, "Our other heater is at the 818th Medical Battalion with our Flight Medic SSG Crispin Perez."

Later, CPT Babine came around and said, "Stand-To is at 0600 hours (6 am) in the morning. Be in MOPP Level 1 in the chow line."

This evening, I got SSG Crispin Perez and SSG Lucia Gabriela's next of kin information.

Also, I received a beautiful Christmas card from Joe Clark and his family (my wife Cindy's brother).

Day 49: 21 Jan 1991 / Monday

We had Red Dragon Alert several times last night and early this morning. The First Sergeant instructed us to get into MOPP Level 1; go in and out of the tents and bunkers several times.

It was broadcasting over the radio that Iraq Scud missiles had launched for Dhahran Saudi Arabia, Riyadh, Saudi Arabia, and Bahrain. They were all intercepted, except for one that went into the ocean.

This morning the sky is dark with no beautiful stars. There have not been any stars showing since the night of the attack on 17 Jan 1991. We are all exhausted today from all the alerts and not getting much sleep last night and early morning. It is now 0540 hours (5:40 am), and it is pouring down rain.

SGT Red volunteers to pull detail today. Later he informed me, "I need off detail to go pick up Medical Supply."

Later this morning, CPT Babine asked me to list Medical Equipment shortages, so I gave it to him. SSG Sims is Day First-up on AC # 736. He already had a mission this morning, and it is now 1035 hours (10:35 am). Also, I got word; we have a new captain aviator in our unit today, CPT Diane Sander.

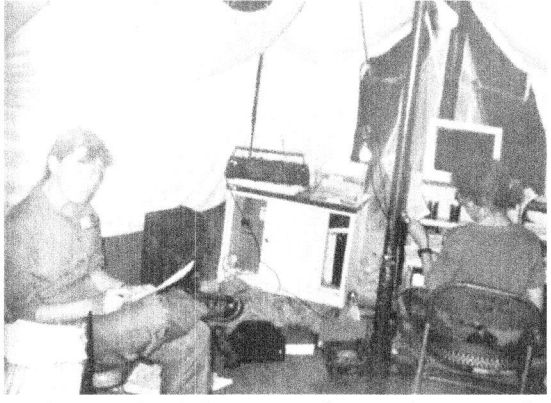

Setting on the left is one of our pilots. On the right is SGT Penny Suazo.

The First Sergeant asked me today to say a few words about SSG Hailey in the Memorial Service. It is scheduled for him tomorrow at 1300 hours (1 pm).

This afternoon SGT Penny Suazo and I took the Blazer vehicle to the 818th Medical Battalion to pick up SSG Hailey's personal belongings. While there, SGT Penny Suazo got SSG Schaberg signed paperwork to accompany SSG Hailey's body back to Germany. She also brought back some mail to our company.

I brought back a red heater that I signed for a while ago. We needed it here at our main camp, as our potbelly stove in our tent has been acting up.

We left the 818th Medical Battalion after dark. We had to use a blackout drive until we got on the main road. Also, we had to switch to a blackout drive when we got close to the airfield. I sure do hate driving in a blackout. It is so hard to see.

This evening, I received the package with all the goodies I had asked Cindy to send me. I received my electric blanket (that I can hook up to the electrical cable going to our tent from the generators), two razors, one with batteries, one electric, a letter from Cindy, and Christmas Cards. She mailed it to me on 29 Dec 1990. I sure was glad to receive it all.

After that, I wrote Cindy a letter thanking her for the package and letter. Then I read all the Christmas Cards. It was after midnight when I went to sleep.

Day 50: 22 Jan 1991 / Tuesday

I slept pretty well using the electric blanket last night. I am glad we did not have any Stand-To or Red Dragon all night, like the night before. We had Stand-To at 0600 hours (6 am). Then we are released until the 0730 hours (7:30 am) Company Formation.

I shaved this morning with the electric razor Cindy sent me. I'm glad she sent it to me along with the batteries operated shaver that I keep in my ammo pouch on my LBE. Also, she sent me socks, grey physical training shorts & jacket, goodies along with a letter she wrote on 29 Dec 1990.

This morning I took SSG Hailey's personal belongings out of the M-6 Blazer vehicle and brought them into, CPT Babine tent. There CPT Babine, SSG Diane Riggins, and I took inventory of SSG Hailey's personal belongings before they shipped out to KKMC. CPT Babine informed me, "SSG Clint would accompany SSG Hailey's body. Major Becker (Commander) advises me, he will need all the Flight Medics he has for combat."

We had hot chow at 1130 hours (11:30 am). After I ate, I laid down for a little while to get some rest. The weather is quite cold today.

SSG Garland Hailey Memorial Service at 1300 hour (1 pm) on 22 Jan 1991.

We had the Memorial Service for SSG Hailey today at about 1300 hours (1 pm). I was also one of the Soldiers who was supposed to say something, but I did not get called to come up. I probably would have gotten all choked up anyway. It was a sad day. A lot of Soldiers got up and talked some about SSG Hailey. I remember SSG Niles said a few words and then open up his canteen and poured water on the ground. He said, "This is for our falling comrade."

I know I am going to miss SSG Hailey. Losing one of the service members of my platoon is the most challenging point in my military career. I know it was hard on a lot of Soldiers. I have to find strength and move on. After the Memorial Service, I went for a walk alone around the perimeter of the airfield. I felt sad, and I talked to God and asked him for the strength to carry on.

In the Staff Meeting at 1800 hours (6 pm), our Commander said, "Two Iraq Scud missiles intercepted by the Patriot (Phased Array Tracking Radar to Intercept On Target, Scud Busters) real close to the Port. The security at the Port is very tight now. They are always in MOPP Level 1 all the time."

CPT Babine came by and filled me in on the aircraft committed for tomorrow. Later, First Sergeant showed me the rating scheme. He told me, "I will make you a copy of it." Then he said, "SSG James would be the First Squad

Leader to replaced SSG Hailey." After he left, I fixed a can of roast beef that Cindy sent me. I also made a cup of hot cocoa. It was good too. After I finish eating, I went to sleep.

Day 51: 23 Jan 1991 / Wednesday

I slept well last night with my electric blanket. Last night was the first night I slept without my flight suit on since 15 Jan 1991. Well, today is my brother Tommy's birthday. He is 35 years old today.

SGT Homer said at about 0558 hours (5:58 am), "SFC Taylor, "We have Company Formation in about 2 minutes." I jumped out of my cot, put on my flight suit, LBE, protective mask, weapon, helmet, and just made it on time. The only one missing was SSG Davis. SSG Davis has detail duty for today.

Today, two Soldiers from each platoon were able to go for the AT&T Phone Call Run. I pick SGT Homer and SGT Gold. SGT Kerwin wanted to go, but he has Day First-up. He also said, "I need to wash my clothes today." I later got SGT Kerwin's next of kin's address to send to Cindy, so she can keep his wife informed. Cindy is fantastic as the Wife Support Channel. She is very supportive of the Soldier's wives and me.

CPT Babine asked me for two Soldiers to help Maintenance install the armor cavalier floor platting (protect from enemy fire) on the helicopters. Later, I washed my clothes from 1130 hours (11:30 am) until 1300 hours (1 pm). SSG Davis borrowed some soap powder from me to wash his clothes.

At about 1700 hours (5 pm), I took the first hot shower I had in a while. It felt terrific. Those guys did an excellent job in closing the six shower stalls. Only three have the fuel immersion heater (heat the water) in the shower booths. The shower stalls have floors, seats to set on, walls on all four sides with a plastic roof.

After I took my shower, I changed into a clean flight suit and went to the Staff Meeting. At the meeting, our Commander said, "There will be NO hot shower until all showers are working." Then he said, "It is the same Soldiers every day taking a shower." I think it is his way of saying, "If I don't take a hot shower, no one does." He also brought up in the meeting, "No more packages will be ship to or from Germany to Saudi Arabia. Also, only up to 12 ounces will be mail out, to include films, cassettes, etc." Our Commander continues by saying, "The ground war starts four to ten days from now, and combat starts in a couple of days."

Today Flight Platoon assignments are as follow:
The First-up Day is AC # 969 with SSG Denzel.
The First-up Night is AC # 736 with SSG Miller.
Training flight is AC # 986 with SSG Davis with a take-off time of 0900 hours (9 am).

Our Commander said, "SSG Clint is in charge of refilling our water supply daily. ALSE is moving tomorrow. The day after the move, they will start checking the flight helmet and flight vest. The MASA (Military Air Staging Area, place assembled for Troops and equipment) will be located here at the airfield for all incoming and outgoing aircraft, coming in or leaving from Germany, or the USA."

Then our Commander said, "We all need to check our bunkers and fighting positions.

Our new sister unit will be the 273rd Medical Company from now on. Also, there will be a promotion board at Battalion in February." Then the Commander said, "The password for tomorrow is 'Drug Store / Transplant.'"

The NBC NCO said, "Not to use the second Ice Pack until directed to do so, as there is no resupply of them.

Our First Sergeant said, "I will start adding the Crew Members to the guard roster." I told First Sergeant, "With the way aircraft changes all the times, that will cause a problem with a Flight Medics having guard duty one day and leaving the next day to go TDY." First Sergeant said, "The Guard duty has priority."

I talked with SSG Denzel tonight about SSG James becoming the First Flight Squad Leader and moving over to his tent. SSG Denzel said, "There is no room in our tent." I asked him, "How many Soldiers are living in your tent?" He said, "There are seven counting SSG Clint." I informed SSG Denzel, "Second Flight Squad tent has a total of nine Soldiers, and once SSG James moves to your tent, there will be an even eight Soldiers in each tent." SSG Denzel said, "I am going to talk with the First Sergeant." I informed SSG Denzel, "I talked with the First Sergeant last night, and he said it was up to SSG James.

Then I told SSG Denzel, "SSG James wants to move to your tent." My thoughts, every time SSG Denzel disagrees with me, he says he is going to talk with the First Sergeant.

CPT Babine stops by the second flight squad tent to update us before heading over to the officer tent to sleep. A little while later, SGT Walling came to me with a desire to use the phone tomorrow. He said, "I need to call my parents to straighten out a problem."

Day 52: 24 Jan 1991 / Thursday

I got a good night's sleep last night. We had a Stand-To formation at 0600 hours (6 am) this morning. One person from each platoon is allowed to go on the phone run this morning. I picked SGT Walling from our platoon. SSG Denzel chose SSG Nile for Detail Duty. No one from the second flight squad is pulling PMCS, as the second flight squad no longer owns a military vehicle.

SGT Walling photo during Operation Desert Storm 1991.

SGT Walling wanted to talk to me. He said, "A few of the guys are picking on me because you choose me to make a phone call run." I told him, "If they want to complain to someone, they need to come to see me." We talked for a while before he left for the phone run.

"A Soldier's Guide Saudi Arabia," I sent this to my son Jonathan on 24 Jan 91.

I wrote a letter to Cindy, Penny, Joy, and Jonathan and enclosed a booklet, "A Soldier's Guide to Saudi Arabia." I had a few extra in my precession.

I asked SGT Homer to take the trash out today and clean the heater. Later he took the garbage out without any problem, but I had to remind him again about cleaning the heater. SGT Homer said, "SFC Taylor, I don't see why I have to clean the heater." I told him, "Because I told you too." Then he started complaining, and I told him, "Just clean the heater and stop complaining."

I like SGT Homer, but he sure does like to complain a lot. I care for all my Soldiers, but being a leader, I have to make some tough decisions that may not be favorable to everyone. This afternoon, I counseled SGT Homer on his behavior and gave him a written formal counsel statement to sign. He did not like it, but he finally signed it.

I returned the bike to Supply since no one in the platoon was using it. SSG Diane Riggins returned my hand receipt on the bicycle. Then she gave me an orange sleeping mat and had me sign for it. I mention to SSG Diane Riggins, "My back sure has been bothering me." She said, "My back is giving me problems too."

I left the Supply tent and saw SGT Denman. We talked for about 1 hour about different things. After that, I went to the Staff Meeting from 1800 hours (6 pm) until 2015 hours (8:15 pm). It was 2 hours and 15 minutes long. It was way too long of a meeting. Our Commander said, "So far, all Iraq Scuds have no chemical weapons. The Iraqi usually launch 10 Scuds missiles per night. Also, we usually only get 20 to 30 minutes warning."

The tomorrow assignments for the flight medics are:
Day First-up is SSG Denzel.
Night First-up is SSG Miller.
Training Flight is SSG Niles.
SGT Gold will make the phone call run.
SSG Davis will be Sergeant of the Guard.
SSG Mullen returned from TDY today and SGT Kerwin will replace him. Now SGT Kerwin is back on his assigned aircraft.

The First Sergeant has given each platoon a responsibility:
Flight Medics will have the duty of Sergeant of the Guards.
Headquarter Platoon duty is KP (Kitchen Police, the detail in the kitchen).
Operation Platoon duties are the Latrine.
Maintenance Platoon will pull Guard Duty.

I also received five letters from Cindy and two letters from Jonathan today. This evening I ate an MRE before I went to bed. It is getting late, time now 2337 hours (11:37 pm), almost midnight. I am tired, and my back hurts.

Day 53: 25 Jan 1991 / Friday

I slept well last night. I got up at 0500 hours (5 am). We had a Stand-To formation at 0600 hours (6 am). The flight medic's assignments for today are as follow:
SGT Gold will go on the phone call run today.
SSG Niles has a training flight.
SSG Miller is Night First-up, and
SSG Denzel is Day First-up.
I told the guys and gal in platoon formation to quit complaining and talking negatively.

Our Commander talked with all the flight medics and pilots. He spoke about how it was at Landstuhl, Germany, and how it will be here. He said, "It is going to be run by rank." After formation, we had a hot breakfast.

SSG Crispin Perez and SSG Lucia Gabriela returned today from TDY. SSG James also returned today from TDY. No one went to the phone call run this morning, and I don't know why. Maybe it is canceled. I informed SSG James, he will be going over to the first flight squad as their squad leader. Then SSG Lucia Gabriela said, "I outrank SSG James."

Therefore, I sent SSG Lucia Gabriela to let CPT Babine know. After that, I gave SSG James and SSG Lucia Gabriela their date of rank to CPT Babine. CPT Babine went and talked with the Commander as the First Sergeant was gone. The Commander wanted to see the proof for each Soldier. SSG Lucia Gabriela nor SSG James had the evidence of their date of rank with them, and Admin did not have it either. Later, I talked with our First Sergeant, and he said, "SSG Lucia Gabriela is the first flight squad leader."

I went to the Staff Meeting tonight at 1800 hours (6 pm). CPT Connell said before the start of the meeting, "Real quick" (before the Commander had a chance to say anything.), "Let's do the other Soldiers first and get them out of here before we conduct our meeting." Our Commander said, "Good idea." Then the Commander started his Staff Meeting. Our Commander said, "Landstuhl,

Germany Post Office is only allowing mail packages to Saudi Arabia no bigger than a shoebox-size or smaller. Also, LTC Love will be here soon, so take the unit patch off your uniforms tonight. Someone suggested using M9 Chemical Paper to cover up the patch. Then someone else said, "The 12th Evac Hospital expects 1,000 patients a day." Our Commander said, "Each medevac unit is authorized one 5,000 gallon water truck.

Photo of our Company 5,000-gallon water truck.

I requested a vehicle for SSG Crispin Perez for his eye appointment. SSG Clark said, "SGT Janet Flatau (she is married to SGT Thomas Flatau, both are in this unit, but sleep in separate tents) needs a ride for Sick Call too.

CPT Connell said, "The 101st Airborne Division is tearing down camp and moving out tonight." Then he said, "We will have to defend ourselves." Our Commander said, "I was giving information about a possible air attack. Also, General McFarland said, to salute out here." Then Our Commander said, "Just to salute officers in other units and not me."

Someone mention, "A Soldier, got 2nd degree burned with a kerosene stove heater and caught the tent on fire." Then Mr. (CW2) Price said, "No to any desert boots with the flight suit."

Our Commander said, "No co-ed in the shower, even with permission." The Commander also wants to know who wants wood or grass carpet floors? I informed our Commander, "The second flight squad wants grass carpet on our floor."

At the end of the Staff Meeting, our Commander said, "Did you notice? I did as CPT Connell suggested. I went from bottom to top, and everyone still here." CPT Connell then suggested, "We can have the Staff Meeting at 1700 hours (5 pm) or 1730 hours

(5:30 pm) instead." Our Commander said, "We tried it, and it did not work."

I looked at the Commander and said, "0600 hours (6 am)." The Commander did not say anything. Then, our Commander said, "We have the meeting at 0600 hours (6:00 am)." Then he said, "We have Stand-To at 0600 hours (6 am) and Staff Meeting at 0630 hours (6:30 am)." It was the first time the Commander accepted what I suggested. I was amazed and also quite pleased that he listens to me and is giving it a try. Before we left the meeting, they gave us the password for tomorrow. The Password is "Sermon and Orange."

After the meeting, I went back to our tent and brief the second flight squad. Then, I took SSG Lucia Gabriela to the first flight squad tent and introduced her to her new section. Then I brief the first flight squad. SSG Lucia Gabriela asked her new team, "If you don't mind, I would like to move my personal belongings to the front right side of the tent." They said, "You're the squad leader." My thought, hopefully, everything will work out for the best as it should.

Day 54: 26 Jan 1991 / Saturday

Today we had a Stand-To formation at 0600 hours (6 am). SGT Homer performed the duty of Second Squad Leader position as SSG Crispin Perez is off today. SSG Crispin Perez, SSG Lucia Gabriela, and SSG James had the day off for TDY return, which I granted. SSG Mullen has Sergeant of the Guard at 0900 hours (9 am). So he is allowed to sleep in this morning.

SSG Miller had Night First-up but did not have any mission last night, so he is Day First-up today. We have no Night First-up today as the 273rd Medical Company will pull that duty. SSG Crispin Perez will dispatch a vehicle at 0630 hours (6:30 am) to go to his 0730 hours (7:30 am) eye doctor's appointment. SGT Janet Flatau will go with SSG Crispin Perez to sick call.

We had the Staff Meeting at 0630 hours (6:30 am). It works out great. Our Commander went through things quickly and then said, "Everyone else is release, except for those who have their reports to turn in."

SSG Lucia Gabriela moved over to the first flight squad tent today. The first flight squad even helped her with her move. They surprised her with a welcome card and balloons. SSG James moved over to her corner she had in the second flight squad tent. Today I gave SSG Lucia Gabriela her initial formal counsel statement of what I expect of her as a squad leader for the first flight squad. I have already written one for the second flight squad leader, SSG Crispin Perez but have not had the chance to give it to him.

Today, we removed everything out of the second flight squad tent. We laid down the green artificial turf carpet on our floor. That makes it a lot better to walk on.

It was nice not having to go to the Staff Meeting tonight. 1LT Bryant got a few people together and put up the recreation tent. I would of help, but I was busy fixing up my tent and AO.

I walked over and took a nice cold shower, as we cannot get a hot shower until all the shower booth has hot water and plenty of it, per our Commander. Well, anyway, there are no waiting lines to take a shower, which made it pleasant. The inside shower dressing area cut the wind down and gave more room to dress and undress. The water was freezing, but I did do 50 push up before taking my shower to get my body warmed up. Anyway, I feel good being clean, even though I almost got frostbit in Saudi Arabia! Then I went back to the tent and relaxed.

Later SSG Mullen gave me a Star & Strip Newspaper for the 16 Jan 1991. I started to read it until I got two letters from Cindy. She wrote those letters on 27 Dec 1990 and 10 Jan 1991. It was great to hear from her.

CPT Babine came into the tent and told me the status of the aircraft for tomorrow. He said AC # 001 is going to Dhahran tomorrow in SSG Crispin Perez bird, but he has an eye appointment to check his new disposable contact lens at the 12the Evac Hospital. So SSG Miller said, "I will take the flight to Dhahran as I need to pick up the NVG." Then CPT Babine said, "AC # 736, SSG Miller bird has Day First-up," and SSG James spoke up, "I will pull it for SSG Miller."

CPT Babine said, "Presently, I have two pilots and one flight medic, and I need two more flight medics. They need five Soldiers from each platoon for perimeter guards."

Later, CPT Babine came back and said, "The flight medic that is going to Dhahran can pick up small items at the PX for the flight medics, and the crew chief can do the same for the crew chiefs. I gave SSG Miller four dollars and a list of 2 items, Q-tips and clothes hangers. He said, "Is that an order?" He is making a big deal of it, so I told him, "Just forget it." It makes me sick to have a crybaby NCO in my platoon.

I went to sleep at about 2030 hours (8:30 pm). I slept pretty well too. It rains during the night and is still raining.

Day 55: 27 Jan 1991 / Sunday

I woke up this morning, and it is still raining and hard. I heard SSG Miller up and around getting ready for his flight. I don't know if they will fly with all this rain. SSG Lucia Gabriela stopped by at 0622 hours (6:22 am) and said, "I am the only one for Stand-To around the perimeter." I informed her, "There are two other pilots."

Well, they change the 0630 hours (6:30 am) Staff Meeting until after the 0800 hours (8 am) Company Formation. I wish I had known that. I would have slept in a little longer. This morning I talked with SSG Crispin Perez and SSG Lucia Gabriela. It seems SSG Davis is pulling Sergeant of the Guard every other day and is causing a moral issue among the Soldier in the platoon. After talking with my two squad leaders, I will stop that. Now I will go by the Duty Roster (DA Form 6) given flight duty priority.

They needed a flight medic for SSG Davis bird. So I volunteered to go. While in flight, the helicopter windshield crack got larger. So Mr. (CW2) Young decided to return to home base. I got six hours of flight time. After we landed, I turned in my flight helmet and flight vest to Aviation Life Support Equipment, as it has not had an inspection yet.

CPT Babine said, "I need to see all flight medics in the Operation tent." There he briefs both the pilots and flight medics on the battle crews and the chain of command.

Later, SSG Lucia Gabriela suggested to me, "It would be a good idea to have the squads meeting altogether. This way, we can work out any differences we have." I said, "Okay," then I told both squad leaders independently we will have a meeting tomorrow.

After that, I went back to my tent and fixed myself a ham slices MRE with some pita bread. It was pretty good fixed up like that. Also, I talked with the guys some in our tent. Then SSG Schaberg came by and spoke with the second flight squad some too.

Today, CPT Babine came into our tent and briefed me on the flights for tomorrow as follow:
AC # 969 has Training Flight at 1500 hours (3 pm) with SSG Denzel.
AC # 726 will be Day Second-up with SSG Niles.
AC # 730 will be leaving for Ranco (place in Riyadh, Saudi Arabia) take-off time 1000 hours (10 am) with SGT Walling.
AC # 736 will cover for Day First-up until 0900 hours (9 am) with SGT Homer.

AC # 746 has NVG at 1900 hour (7 pm) with SSG James.

AC # 001 has Overnight night to Dhahran with SSG Miller.

I went to sleep tonight at 2130 hours (9:30 pm).

Day 56: 28 Jan 1991 / Monday

We had a Stand-To formation at 0600 hours (6 am) this morning. I got up about 15 minutes before, but I made it on time. I went to the Staff Meeting at 0630 hours (6:30 am). It was over at 0700 hours (7 am). I am glad that the meeting has changed. I see it as a significant improvement. The information is accurate and up to date. Plus, the info is getting out to the Soldiers faster, and the reports are up to date.

I went to get a hot breakfast, and when I return to our tent, I realized it was 0720 hours (7:20 am). So I put my meal on my table and went to Company Formation. Before the formation started, I put out the information from the Staff Meeting.

After formation, I went back to our tent and ate my breakfast. Later, CPT Connell stopped by our tent. He said, "All the fight medics need to take one of their blankets from their blanket set and find some way of tying it over the helicopter windshields. We need to protect the windshield from the loose gravel hitting the windshield, causing it to crack when another helicopter is taking off or hovering to land.

I just put a blanket over the hanger queen's windshield (helicopter always broke down for one reason or the other) AC # 756. I tied it down with ropes. I assisted SSG Denzel in putting a blanket on his AC # 956 windshield and securing it down under the windshield wipers blades and front doors.

I talked to SGT Homer in private. Finally, he opens up to me, and we discussed the problem. He feels he is the only E-5 (SGT), which is correct in the second flight squad and gets picked on; that he cannot run his additional duty as Company Standardization with Battalion Standardization NCO here in the Second Squad tent. So we talked about these things for a while.

Later, SSG James and I talked about my aid bags, medical equipment, and IV's sets. He said, "I use mast trouser (Military Anti-Shock Trousers, are medical devices used to treat severe blood loss and maintain blood level) on one of the two men that got stuck by a 2 ½ ton truck."

I later worked on SGT Homer EER. Then I read some on IV from a book SSG James loan me. I worked on SSG Mullen EER too. Also, I counsel SSG Mullen for his Quarterly Formal Counsel Statement. I can always depend on SSG Mullen. He never gives me any trouble and still does what I ask or more.

A Formal Counsel Statement is something I do with all my Soldiers. I give them an Initial Formal Counsel Statement of what I expect of them. Each quarter, I make another Formal Counsel Statement to let them know how well they meet or exceed those requirements. Then I go into areas where they need to work more to improve their weakness.

The electrical power went off today. So it was hard to see to write in my diary. I help the guys straighten up the area of SSG Sims.

I worked on the gauge to the small heater. At about 1700 hours (5 pm), I walked over and took a warm shower. It felt pretty good too. When I got back to our tent, I open up one of the cans of chunky ham that Cindy had sent me. I heated it for my supper.

At 1830 hours (6:30 pm), the Flight Platoon went to the company training on Challenge and Password. After the class, I had all the flight medics come outside to the side of the second flight squad tent so we can get things out in the open. I told them about the new structures and what I expect from them. Then SSG Davis said, "The First Sergeant tent had the heater on, and no one was in the tent." SGT Gold said, "I lost my helmet for four days, and everyone was on my case." SGT Homer said, "SFC Inniss stands up for his Soldiers, but we don't see that of you." I then told them, "I do stand up for my Soldiers, but I don't do it in public. I do it in private." They said, "You should let us know, even if you lose."

After that, SSG Denzel brought up, "When the Company first organized, the Commander decided to split the platoon into two flight platoons; when it should be one flight platoon like it is now according to TOE (Table of Organization and Equipment)."

SSG James brought up, "When I return to the tent from the latrine, you told me I must be in full dress uniform, helmet, LBE, and protective mask." He said, "I see lots of other Soldiers in other platoons, not in uniforms, even the First Sergeant."

Then, Soldiers in the Second Flight Squad tent started complaining and said, "We don't even like to be in the tent with you, as you always find something for us to do. We preferred to go TDY." Then someone said, "Telling us over and over again to take the trash out." I told them, "I came to a decision this morning to let Second Flight Squad Leader, SSG Crispin Perez, run this tent, and I run the platoon. SGT Homer said, "Since we talked, we worked out our difference." I felt like he was satisfied. I told them all, "We will get back together in a couple of weeks to talk again. I care for every one of you, and I give you all 100% of my support."

After the meeting, SSG Mullen, SSG Crispin Perez, and I watch one of SSG Mullen war movie in the Recreation tent.

After the meeting, SSG Mullen, SSG Crispin Perez, and I left to watch one of the war movies that belong to SSG Mullen in the Recreation tent. I watch some of it until I decided it was getting late. Plus, I did not have the aircraft numbers, flights for First-up, Second-up flight medics, or Sergeant of the Guard assignments. I walked into the Operation tent, and nothing was on the mission board.

I went to look for CPT Babine, and he had nothing. I talked to him about the meeting with my platoon and how it turned into a complaining section. He said, "Sometimes it is good to have those meetings." CPT Babine was very understanding about it.

Later, CPT Babine came by the tent and told me AC # 735 would be First-up tomorrow with Flight Medic SGT Gold. I went to the First Flight Squad tent to inform SGT Gold that he has First-up tomorrow and fill the other flight medics of the recent information. Those there started asking me for clarification on the about 25% of the tent Soldiers have to pull Stand-To! Then SSG Denzel asked me, "Where Stand-To Soldiers go?" I told them, "This is all news to me too. I will check and let you all know."

I went to talk with CPT Dodson, CPT Babine, CPT Connell, and CPT Diane Sanders. It was hard to get a straight answer from any of them. Finally, CPT Babine said, "For the Stand-To Soldiers to go to their bunker or see the Sergeant of the Guard," which is SSG Lucia Gabriela tonight.

I went to both tents to inform them where to go for Stand-To. SGT Homer volunteer to pull Stand-To for the second flight squad as we only have four Soldiers in our tent tonight.

After all that, I went to my cot and went to sleep.

Day 57: 29 Jan 1991 / Tuesday

I slept pretty well last night. I went to the Staff Meeting at 0630 hours (6:30 am). They still did not have anything written on the aircraft status board this morning. I suggested to our Commander, "Sir, I recommend one-day before having the information on the mission board." Our Commander quickly shot that down by saying, "That is a platoon leader function." I felt why in the world I'm sitting in here if they don't even listen to me. Our Commander said, "There is a class tomorrow night, 'Rule of Engagement,' at 1830 hours (6:30 pm)."

The NBC NCO said, "The MOPP Suit is not to be wear as a wet or cold weather uniform." Our Commander said, "Good point, mixing uniforms not allowed." CPT Connell said, "We should feel our electric cord going into our tents to see if it is hot." No one gave a response to what CPT Connell suggested.

Our Commander asked me, "Why all the helicopters not covered with blankets?" I quickly said, "They will be today." CPT Swingle said, "Good answer SFC Taylor." Our Commander brought up the subject, "Sex in the field is punish under UCMJ (Uniform Code of Military Justice) Article 15 (Military formal punishment). There will be no holding hands, kissing, touching, and etcetera." Our Commander continues to say, "Pregnancy female will get an Article 15."

I asked the questions that our Soldiers wanted an answer to, such as LES (Leave Earning Statement, pay statement) and cashing checks. Mr. (WO1) Gambrel said, "I will check on it."

After the meeting, I went to the aircraft to check the status of the aircraft blankets. To see which aircraft did not have one on them. Later, the First Sergeant had a meeting. He changed the uniform three times that can be wear to the shower and restroom. Now we wear our weapons and carry our protective masks. He talked about Sex in the field. He then said, "There an E-4 and E-6 getting it on hot and heavy." The First Sergeant said, "The female Soldier assigned to the 273rd Medical

Company and was ordered by her Commander not to leave her camp to come over here to see a specialist, not giving out no name. Well, she did anyway, so now she is attached to another company."

Our First Sergeant said, "We will have Stand-To every 3rd day by the platoon." He said, "Each platoon can use the washer machine every 3rd day." Later, the Commander wanted all flight medics to stand by their helicopters.

Someone has been making fighting positions with the bulldozer they found on the side of the road. They hot-wired it and brought it back to our camp. Also, today, we had hot food for lunch.

I went flying today on AC # 726 as AC # 736 changed at the last minute, and I flew for 2.9 hours. CPT Diane Sanders was having a lot of trouble landing, and it scared me. Later, talking with the Crew Chief SPC John Hasselius, he stated his helicopter had trim issues to contribute to her challenges. I notice while flying tonight, there is a lot of green spots of grass in the desert.

When we returned, I went back to my tent and fixed a can of Chunky Turkey with bread. I made some pink lemonade too. Also, I received two sweet letters from Mom # 5 and # 6. She wrote them on the 2nd and 5th of Jan 1991. I am fixing to go to bed now as I am exhausted.

SPC John Hasselius, Crew Chief on UH-60 Medivac Blackhawk Helicopter. Courtesy photo from John Hasselius.

Day 58: 30 Jan 1991 / Wednesday

I slept well last night, and I did not want to get up this morning. I went to the Staff Meeting at 0630 hours (6:30 am). There they talked about Intelligent Reports. The person giving the talk said, "Two Iraqi soldiers are capture, and they waved a white sheet of paper. The Iraqi soldiers only had one gas mask. Other reports are that they only get one meal a day, their morale is terrible, 50% will quit, and some have already left to go to other countries.

A terrorist from Pakistan driving a blue sedan with a Jordan license plate is capture that was going to bomb a US bus. Also was brought up, our water supply is also their target." Our Commander said, "None of this information from the Staff Meeting is to be written in letters sending back home or talk about over the telephone."

Our Commander said, "SSG Lucia Gabriela is going on emergency leave today." Then our Commander said, "Anymore writing on the latrine wall, I will put a latrine guard there." Also, the Commander said, "An Alpha Roster is out, the last name beginning in A – L take a shower on odd days, and M – Z on even days. Next month it will flip flops. In other words, every other day, we can take a shower."

Commander said, "Stand-To with the Flight Platoon from 0600 – 0645 hours (6 am – 6:45

am). Better yet, make it from 0600 – 0700 hours (6 am – 7 am)." Then someone said, "Hot breakfast is tomorrow." The Commander replied, "Change it back to 0600 – 0645 hours (6 am – 6:45 am)."

SFC Inniss said someone took SPC Alicia Phillips's sleeping bag off the clothesline and left their dirty sleeping bag in its place. Her sleeping bag smells like Jergens Lotion. I can pick out the smell." Commander said, "Have everyone stand in Company Formation with their sleeping bag, and SFC Inniss will smell each one."

Our company clotheslines. Photo courtesy of Jim Mullen.

I gave the First Sergeant a copy of SSG Crispin Perez's promotion order promoting him to the rank of E-7 (Sergeant First Class). I informed the First Sergeant, his wife sent it to him. I also asked the First Sergeant to have the Commander present this to him in Company Formation today as he has NVG tonight.

This morning, before formation, SSG James and SGT Gold left for the phone run. It is SGT Gold wedding anniversary today.

At Company Formation, everyone was standing with their sleeping bag. Our Commander said, "The sleeping bag matter has been resolve."

Our Commander called, "SSG Crispin Perez, "Front and Center" (Military command to take one step backward, do a right face, and report in front of the Commander, salute and say, "Report as directed"). In Company Formation, the Commander removed SSG Crispin Perez E-6 Strip and pinned on his new E-7 Strip in front of the company, promoting him to Sergeant First Class.

After the formation, I went and checked the five fighting position for tomorrow. Later, SGT Red asked for help with Medical Supply.

SGT Homer, SSG Mullen, and I gave SGT Red a helping hand.

At 1200 hours (noon), SSG Denzel, SPC William, and I went to the 5 – 10 KW Generator and Pump Class. SFC Forest taught the class. This class is required to use the washer machine on an assigned washer day. It is also necessary to use the pump to fill the shower water tanks and apply power to the electric heat.

After the class, we ate a hot meal. Today, I was able to get the Medical Equipment from AC # 579, the one that crash, to give to SFC Crispin Perez to use on his bird, AC # 001.

Well, today, I took a lukewarm shower that felt like water getting into a swimming pool. Then I put on clean clothes and walk over to the 1800 hours (6 pm) Rules of Engagement class taught by SSG Fox. When the course was over, I mailed a letter to Cindy.

Later, SGT Penny Suazo said, "You got a package, and it is in your tent." I looked in my tent and did not find it. I walked to the Operation tent, but no one there had any packages there for me. Then I walked over to the Admit tent and talked with SGT Penny Suazo; she said, "I gave it to SSG James." So I walked back to our tent, and on the way, I saw SSG James. I called out to him, "SSG James." He said, "Your box is next to my cot." When I got back to our tent, I opened up my package and found three Star & Strips Newspapers dated 19 Jan 1991, 20 Jan 1991, and 23 Jan 1991. Also, a can of brownies Cindy made, a bag of the chip with dip, Hot Cocoa mix, a large can of Tuna, and a package of Girl Scout Cookies. Also, letters from Cindy dated 24 Jan 1991, one from Moe's wife, one from SFC Cortez Cunningham, and a letter from my Mother.

In the letter, Cindy wrote, "I did not sleep at all on Thursday, 17 Jan 1991." That was the morning of the attack against Iraq. In her letter, she said, "SSG Hailey's Memorial Service was on the 25 Jan 1991."

Before I went to sleep, CPT Babine brought me three letters from "Any Service Members." One was from a 12 years old girl named Laura Johnson, who lives in Spokane, Washington. She had written to me before. I went to sleep at about 2230 hours (10:30 pm).

On the back of the photo reads, "To Dewey, this is me. I love baseball, at Age 11."

Day 59: 31 Jan 1991 / Thursday

I got up at 0500 hours (5 am), got ready, and made myself a cup of hot mocha. I made it with the can of cocoa mix Cindy had sent me. The Flight Platoon had Stand-To at 0600 hours (6 am) this morning. We all met in front of the Warrant of Arabia Tent (Warrant Officer Tent). There we were broken down into five fighting positions, and the rest of us roam the perimeter.

Photo of officers in front of the Warrant of Arabia tent. From left to right, kneeling is CPT Connell, Mr. Thomas, Mr. Dial, and Mr. Ronan. Standing left to right are Mr. Gambrel, Mr. Fleming, Mr. Anderson, Mr. Hall, and Mr. Young.

At 0630 hours (6:30 am), I went to the Staff Meeting. It went by pretty fast today. Admin Officer said, "SSG Lucia Gabriela caught a C-12 Plane (The C-12 Huron, a twin-turboprop passenger and cargo aircraft, is the military version of the Beechcraft Super King Air) at Ranco yesterday to Dhahran with no waiting time." We had no S-2 (Military Intelligence) news today, except the US forces got the city by the border of Saudi Arabia back. Today is the Flight Platoon day to wash clothes. Our

First Sergeant said, "The shower list starts tomorrow. Company formation today starts at 0800 hours (8 am), as the Dinner Facility did not open until 0700 hours (7 am)."

After Company Formation, I put out information to the Flight Platoon. I told them I have three slots for the Phone run today—one for officer and two for enlisted. Then CPT Babine disagrees with me. He wanted to send more officers. I informed him, "I went to the First Sergeant and fought for that extra slot." The Flight Platoon enlisted did not think that was fair with CPT Babine trying to get our extra slot for my enlisted Soldiers. When CPT Babine returned, I quickly told him, "You needs to let us have at least 1 for the enlisted Soldier." He said, "Do what you want."

After formation, the First Sergeant gave me the names of the five Soldiers who require an EER. He said, "It needs to be done by COB (close of business) today. I told First Sergeant, "No way." He said, "By at least COB tomorrow." I told him, "I do what I can, as I have been busy with everything else."

After that short Staff Meeting, I walked over, cranked up the 5 KW Generator. Then with the water pump, I filled the washer machine tank with water. After that, I did a PMCS on the 10 KW civilian generator. It was a quart and a half low. I check with SSG Tai, and he told me the oil is in the trailer. I open a new five-gallon can of oil and got an empty water bottle to put the oil in. I ended up making two trips to get the oil. After that, I cranked the generator up at 0900 hours (9 am).

Later at about 1030 hours (10:30 am), I washed my clothes in the electric washing machine with a ringer. It was strange using those old fashion washer machines with a clothes ringer. After I finished, I turned off the 5 KW generator, took my clothes to my AO, and hung them out to dry. Then I walk over to get a hot lunch at 1200 hours (noon). I brought the food back to my area of the tent. After I ate, I went to sleep for about half an hour as I was tired.

Our new wash area with two old fashion washer machines and the generator and pump in the background. Photo courtesy of Jim Mullen.

After that, I got up, walk over, and cranked the 5 KW generator so the pilots could wash their clothes. Then with the water pump, I put more water in the washer machine tank. The civilian 10 KW generator ran out of gas, so I poured about eight gallons of gas in it, and I restarted. It did not want to start at first, but it finally did.

I completed SGT Homer EER and turned them to SGT Cauthorn in Admin. Then I walked back to my AO and completed SSG Sims and SSG Mullen EERs. I still need to recopy the EERs and give them to CPT Connell to do his part.

Later, SSG James said, "You could go to supply and sign for an orange mattress for the fight medics." So I signed one for the following Soldiers: SSG James, SSG Sims, SGT Homer, SSG Mullen, SSG Schaberg, SSG Miller, SSG Davis, SSG Lucia Gabriela, and SGT Kerwin.

I got SSG James and SSG Mullen to help me carry the orange mattress back to our tent. I did not get one for SFC Crispin Perez as he already went to supply and signed for his.

The generator has been running from 0900 hours (9 am) to 1700 hours (5 pm), and the water is still lukewarm. After I took a shower, I checked the thermostat, and it's turned up all the way. I read the voltage, and it read 250 – 380 volts. We only have it running at 110 – 120 volts. I felt the heated filament, and it is warm, but not hot like it should be. I think they are not using enough voltage. I also believe this Saudi 10 KW general is a piece of junk like those Saudi bikes.

Day 60: 01 Feb 1991 / Friday

I slept good last night, comfortable and warm. After Company Formation, SSG James and SGT Homer went on the Phone Run to call home with other Soldiers. I went on Sick Call to have my ears check and, most of all, to visit SSG Schaberg. When I got to the 12th Evac Hospital, SPC Garcia and I got off the truck and walked over to the hospital. When I came into SSG Schaberg's ward, I notice he was not there. I asked about him, and they said he had already left to go to PAD (Patient Administration).

So I walked over to PAD and asked for SSG Schaberg. They said, "He hasn't gotten here yet." Then I walked by the EMT (Emergency Medical Treatment) area, and I heard that a cardiac patient was coming. The next thing I knew, a helicopter landed, and I saw a bunch of Soldiers rolling a patient on a gurney (stretcher with attached wheels, use to transport patient) and working on him. Then I notice, the one upfront was SSG Schaberg, who was bagging the patient airway (giving the patient oxygen). SSG Schaberg, before he even got a discharge from being a patient himself, he was back at work saving other people's life.

IV Class with SSG Mullen holding IV bag, SFC Taylor prepares the IV for CPT Babine hand. On the right side of the picture is CPT Babine, and SFC Perez on the left-hand side.

The First Sergeant gave us a ride back to the company from the 12th Evac Hospital. This afternoon, we had a medical class on IV taught by SSG James. He instructs me on giving CPT Babine an IV to his hand, but it did not work. Then SGT Homer tried to do it to the other arm and could not get the IV started. I felt terrible for CPT Babine having to get stuck twice. CPT Babine said, "Have you guys learned anything about this?" I said, "Yes, sir, don't volunteer."

After class, I finish straighten up my AO. Then I took a shower.

SFC Dewey Taylor, Platoon Sergeant, and Senior Flight Medic, inside our tent of the 2nd Flight Squad.

SSG Schaberg on the left and SFC Crispin Perez on our tent's right, of the 2nd Flight Squad.

Later in the tent, I passed out the can of brownies Cindy made and told SSG Schaberg we are welcoming him back. Everyone said the brownies were excellent and to thank Cindy. I wrote Cindy a letter tonight to let her know the news and that my Soldiers liked the brownies she sent.

CPT Babine came into the tent and gave me the status for tomorrow.
SGT Walling has First-up.
SGT Red has Second-up.
SGT Homer has a flight to Riyadh (City in Saudi Arabia).
SGT Gold will be off from being on Sergeant of the Guard.

Day 61: 2 Feb 1991 / Saturday

I slept good last night, nice and warm. I got up at 0530 hours (5:30 am) and went to Staff Meeting at 0630 Hours (6:30 am). This morning, SGT Waldron called attention when our Commander walked in. The Commander liked that. The rest of the officers there said, "He is in the area all the time." Our Commander told SGT Waldron, "You did well."

Someone said, "After Company Formation today, Supply will be picking up body crew armors." Then S-1 (Military Personnel Office) said, "They are working on SSG Hailey's award." Next, they talked about the slow mail because it moves from LBA (Log Base Alpha) to LBE (Log Base Echo).

Our Commander said, "I will talk about the uniform policy tomorrow." Then he read, "Do NOT cut off patients ID (Identification) tags." Then our Commander said the following: "The BX (Base Exchange, store) might be opening up soon, on the other side of the airfield. Sports Day is this afternoon at 1300 hours (1 pm). You can wear tennis shoes and a brown T-shirt."

During the Staff Meeting, CPT Diane Sanders wrote me a note to ask if I had a couple of flight medics that could help them bury telephone cables? I told her, "No, Ma'am."

After the meeting, I went back to my tent and started working on EER. Later, CPT Babine came to me and said, "I want you to provide a couple of fight medics to bury telephone cables." I tried to talk him out of it, but he thinks it would be good for them to see the flight medics doing something. I told him, "We don't want them to get used to seeing us doing detail, as we only pull Sergeant of the Guard." CPT Babine said, "I want a couple of fight medics." I said, "Okay."

I told SSG Mullen to see CPT Babine about burying telephone cables. Then I walk over to the First Fight Squad tent to ask SSG Denzel for a flight medic. He said, "I don't have anyone." I said, "SSG Davis is free." He replied, "How do you know that?" I told SSG Denzel, "I know everyone's status, but I was going to ask you first, as I do not like to micromanage."

I went to my tent and started back working on SSG Mullen and SSG Schaberg EER.

Picture of First Sergeant, SSG Stewart, SSG Schaberg, CW4 Klase, and SFC Crispin Perez playing cards on Sports Day.

We had Sports Day at 1300 hours (1 pm) today. A few of our Soldiers were playing cards, and SSG Mullen was writing a letter. I was working doing my Soldiers EERs.

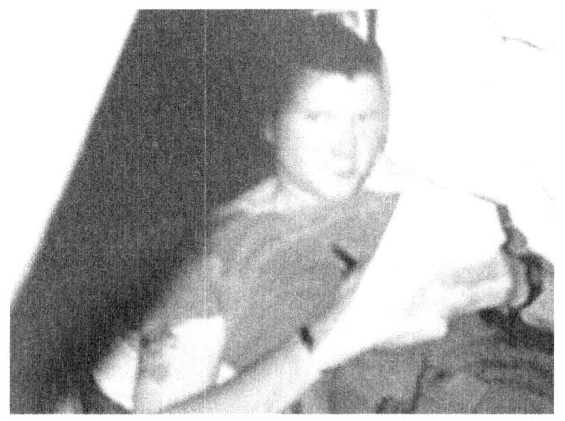

SSG Mullen is writing a letter while lying on his cot during Sports Day. I caught him off guard.

SFC Taylor (Platoon Sergeant) is working on my Soldiers Enlisted Evaluation Reports.

At 1645 hours (4:45 pm), they call for Company Formation. At formation, CPT

Connell (filling in for the Commander's absence) said, "The Blackhawk helicopters are grounded for the next six days or so. Our Battalion grounded them because of reports, parts, and required maintenance." After Company Formation, he had everyone police up around the Maintenance and Supply tents as the General is coming tomorrow.

Later, our First Sergeant stopped by and said, "We have hot breakfast scheduled for tomorrow morning. Also, Stand-To is at 0600 hours (6 am)."

Photo of 2nd Flight Platoon Squad Leader SFC Crispin Perez. He showed me pictures of his wife and three daughters.

SFC Perez told me he talked with his mother today in Puerto Rico and his daughter, who just turned 15 years old today. He also spoke to his wife. Then he showed me a picture of his wife and three daughters. SFC Perez is very proud of his beautiful family.

Now SSG Schaberg is playing a war game of some type. CPT Diane Sanders came in and sat on the floor. She talked to us about the General's visit tomorrow.

Later, I talked with SGT Walling for a while before we walked over and ate a hot lunch. He spoke about his wife and the problems he is having. Tonight, I got my aid bags back from SSG James.

Day 62: 3 Feb 1991 / Sunday

I slept well last night. We had Stand-To this morning from 0600– 0645 hours (6 am - 6:45 am). We had Staff Meeting at 0630 hours (6:30 am). Our Commander put out the following information: "We received Flag Order (Fragmentary Order – change in mission) to Stand Down starting 1200 hours (noon) today for three days due to maintenance. Aircraft from the 818th

Medical BN (Battalion – Over several companies) will be here no later than 0900 hours (9 am).

General McFarlin will be by to check the area unannounced. We need to be prepared for his visit, uniform by policy, and to salute. We are under the microscope, so pay attention to detail. All Soldiers to wear their Kevlar helmets unless they have a medical profile (given medical permission not to wear one) in their pocket, also every vehicle to be painted with the Red Cross and upside-down V."

We had a hot breakfast this morning, and it was good too. Then we had Company Formation at 0800 hours (8 am). There the Commander wanted to see all the crew members in the Recreation tent.

Our First Sergeant told me, "I need two people from the Flight Platoon and Headquarters Platoon. You have a choice between digging fighting positions or spreading barbed wires." I picked spreading barbed wires. I tried to get out of it, but our First Sergeant said, "All of the Maintenance Platoon will be busy." I asked the First

Sergeant, "Do we have a phone run today?" He said, "Yes." Therefore, I asked my platoon who would like to go on the phone run? SSG Niles said, "I would like to go."

SFC Perez, SSG Mullen, and SSG Miller were planning to have their eyes checked. SFC Perez has to return anyway within seven days to have his eyes recheck.

Later, CPT Diane Sanders came to me about SSG Miller and needing time for him to check first aid kits. I said, "He is going to have his eyes checked." After that, CPT Babine wanted to talk to me outside the tent. He chewed me out, but I defended my platoon members and myself. He said, "Those Soldiers going to have their eyes checked are not going. It is for pilots and crew chiefs." He continues to say, "You were in the Staff Meeting when the Commander put the information out." I replied, "I also told the Commander about SFC Perez, having an eye appointment with Colonel Davis." CPT Babine said, "The aircraft has priority. All flight medics are going to inventory the medical equipment and check dates on first aid kits and cold weather kits."

After the talk with CPT Babine, I walked to each aircraft and checked the status. I told each flight medics to give me an inventory of their medical gears.

Later, I talked with SGT Shirt and SPC Garcia. They told me, "We are not allowed to Red X an aircraft we find to be unsafe to fly in the aircraft maintenance logbook, per their Platoon Leader CPT Dodson." Then they said, "CPT Dodson relieved SSG Woolen and SSG Smith for it." I can see the crew chiefs have management problems starting from the platoon leader not allowing their crew chiefs to do their jobs. As a former crew chief myself, I know crew chiefs have that right. After I talked with them, I checked all the fourteen aircraft.

I stopped and talked with the First sergeant and told him we were busy checking the aircraft. He said, "It's alright, I know."

Today, the wind was blowing the sand hard. It was good the two aircraft returned when it did; otherwise, with the poor visibility being as it was, it would have been impossible for helicopters to return to base.

Someone told me I had a box in the Admin tent. I walked over and picked it up. It was a package from Cindy that she sent me on 10 Jan 1991. The package had her blue sleeping bag, box of valentine candy, clothes, 75 watts light bulb, a letter dated 3 Jan 1991, and a card from Eric and Kim Moe. Later, I received another letter from Cindy that she wrote on 15 Jan 1991. It took nineteen days to reach me.

Picture my son Jonathan drew and sent me.

Also, I received a letter from Jonathan, my son, with his school work in it. He is learning a lot, and I am very proud of him. Also, I received a letter from Edna and Dieter from Baumholder, Germany. I spent Christmas with Edna, Dieter, and their two daughters my first tour in Germany in 1976. They said, "We will fix you a German Dinner when you get back and drink wine with us."

I had a hot lunch today. After lunch, I laid down and slept for a little while as I was exhausted. Then I got up, fixed some Mocha, and worked on SSG Miller EER.

SFC Taylor is wearing a blue Ribault Class of 70 T-Shirt that Nancy Mortimer (Classmate) sent me. Here I am drinking a hot cup of Mocha while working on an Enlisted Evaluation Report.

Later, CPT Babine came in, and we talked about everything. He said, "I will allow the flight medics to get their eyes squared away." We talked about the chain of command, maintenance; the crew chief can't put a Red X if they find one on their bird. I told him, "If a crew chief ever refuses to fly with his bird, I am not flying on it, and I am going to advise my flight medics the same." He said, "I don't blame you." He wrote it down and said. "I will check on it."

SSG Sims returned today and said, "I have orders to the 18th Airborne Corp Postal Service out of Dhahran." He was excited. I said, "Show me the orders." He said, "I gave it to the Commander." I heard a couple of guys talking about it yesterday, about making out fake SSG Sim orders. Well, I guess they did it. I did not say anything. It is not my joke.

Later, he told the platoon leader and everybody else, "I'm out of here in a couple of days." I think all the flight medics knew about it but not saying anything. SSG Sims is going to be upset when he finds out this is a joke.

I open up the box of Valentine candy Cindy sent me. I gave some to SSG Schaberg, SGT Homer, and I ate a lot of them. Now everyone else is asleep. I am answering the letter Edna and her husband Dieter, my German friends, wrote to me from Baumholder, Germany. After that, I went to sleep.

Day 63: 4 Feb 1991 / Monday

I got up this morning at 0530 hours (5:30 am). I went to the Staff Meeting at 0630 hours (6:30 am). In the Operation tent, I notice a sign that SSG Sims took from Badsted, Germany.

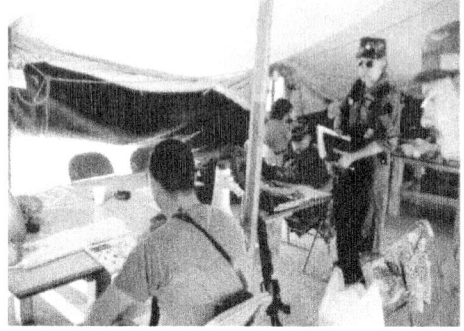

In the Operation tent with our Commander (MAJ Becker) standing up, to the right is our First Sergeant (SFC St. Pierre), the background is SGT Penny Suazo and other unknown. Photo courtesy of Jim Mullen.

In the Saff Meeting, our Commander said, "We will start back flying 7 Feb 1991. Yesterday at 1300 -1400 hours (1 pm – 2 pm), I walked around the aircraft. I noticed covers off the pivot tubes (the cover that protects the pivot tube, connected to the airspeed indicator that read airspeed in knots) and some helicopters not being tied down. I am going to start firing Soldiers if this goes on. Don't paint a rosy picture if it is not."

Then the Commander talked about PMCS that he will be out checking. Our Commander said, "No vehicles dispatch, only mission essential. Also, we are on Maintenance Stand Down, and no phone run today. Classes tomorrow will be OPSEC (Operation Security)."

After Company Formation 0740 hours (7:40 am), the Commander wanted to talk with all the staff folks. He was mostly referring to CPT Babine and CPT Dodson. When they left, I spoke with the First Sergeant about SSG Schaberg needing to go to sick call and eyes checked for a few of my Soldiers who need to go.

Our First Sergeant said, "I will provide a ride for sick call." Then he said, "At 1200 hours (noon), have the Soldiers wanting eyes checked to meet at TOC tent." Later, I informed CPT Babine of an update on all of this.

Today, I was working on the inventory report, and CPT Babine stopped by. He wanted to know if the flight medics are at the aircraft. I said, "Yes, Sir." He wanted to know where SSG Davis and SSG Denzel was? I informed him, "SSG Denzel is doing EER for his Soldiers, and SSG Davis is covering for SGT Walling."

Later, SGT Homer came and got me. He said, "CPT Babine wants to see you in the Motor Pool tent with the First Sergeant." When I got there, CPT Babine asked the First Sergeant and me to go outside the tent. So we went outside the tent. Then CPT Babine started blaming me for allowing Soldiers in my platoon to take care of their eyes. I said, "I informed you." He said, "You did not." I said, "I even wrote it down." Then he said, "That does not prove anything." He started to get me upset with all this. So I called SSG Mullen, SFC Perez, and SGT Walling over to explain the eyes deal with CPT Babine. The First Sergeant did not say anything.

Later, I went out to all the aircraft and checked the equipment. Then I went back to working on the Medical Gear inventory.

We had a class at 1600 hours (4 pm). SSG Miller gave it on the Survival Radio. After the class, CPT Babine wanted to talk to me. He tried to make up with me.

Later, while I was trying to work on SSG Miller EER, CPT Diane Sanders said, "We have a class to go to at 1800 hours (6 pm), five minutes from now." CPT Babine said, "I forgot to inform you." It was a Crew Endurance Class. The class is giving by Mr. (CW2) Price and SSG Clint, and it covered logging time to keep up with crew rest. I did not learn anything, as I was already tired. After the class, CPT Diane Sanders had me get all the flight medics to the second flight squad tent. She gave all the flight medics another level of instruction.

It is now 2030 hours (8:30 pm), and I am going to sleep. I am exhausted, goodnight.

Day 64: 5 Feb 1991 / Tuesday

I got up this morning at 0530 hours (5:30 am). We had Staff Meeting at 0630 hours (6:30 am). Nothing new is put out in the meeting this morning. Then we had Company Formation at 0730 hours (7:30 am). SGT Homer wanted to go to the 12th Evac Hospital to request an instructor to teach Battle Fatigue. Also, he wants to try to get some medical supplies and red crosses while he is there.

I asked CPT Babine, "Would it be alright to allow SSG Miller to go to MEDCOM to have his eyes checked." He said, "I am going to leave that up to you." Therefore, I let him go.

After that, I worked on SSG Miller EER. Then I wrote a few letters. SSG Mullen had Sergeant of the Guard Duty today. SSG Davis volunteers to have Sergeant of the Guard tomorrow.

SSG Davis is sitting at his desk where he does his other duties while not flying.

We had a hot lunch today, and shortly after, I took a short nap. When I got up, I started to repack my two Medical Aid Bags and straightened them out.

At 1900 hours (7 pm), the flight medics and I went to the Operation tent for a class on OPSEC. Mr. (W01) Rios and a Sergeant First Class (I don't remember the name) were teaching the class. There they talk about the Iraqi and other information.

After the class, I came back to my tent and finished packing my aid bags. Then, I cooked an MRE and went to sleep.

Day 65: 6 Feb 1991 / Wednesday

I got up this morning at 0500 hours (5 am). We had Stand-To at 0600 – 0645 hours (6 am – 6:45 am). We had our Staff Meeting at 0630 hours (6:30 am). The Commander said, "I want Medical Supply to order 150 body bags. Also, we have a hot breakfast at 0700 hours (7 am)."

Company formation was at 0800 hours (8 am). I allowed SGT Kerwin, SGT Gold, and SSG Sims to go to the PX and cash their checks. SSG Miller, SGT Walling, and SSG Niles went to MEDCOM to have their eyes checked. SGT Homer went to pick up the doctor with Lieutenant Colonel's rank for the 1300 hour (1 pm) class on Battle Fatigue.

SSG Mullen is standing in front of the 2nd Flight Squad Bunker. Photo courtesy of Jim Mullen.

Today we had a hot lunch at 1200 hours (noon). SGT Homer gave the class on Battle Fatigue, and the doctor was there to answer questions. CPT Dodson did a skit for the course. SFC Inniss thought he was serious. We had the class outside in the sun, behind our tent, and in front of our bunker.

After the class, I went back to my tent, laid down, and got a little rest. SSG Sims had some alcohol free beer and gave me one. I sat and talked with the guys for a little while. The First Sergeant came by and wanted to know who would like to use the phone tomorrow at the 0630 hours (6:30 am) phone run. I told him, "I do, and I will check to see if anyone else in my platoon would like to go." I asked, and no one care to go, but SSG Schaberg said, "I need a ride to sick call in the morning."

While washing my clothes, the General UH-1 Helicopter flew in close by and blowing sand everywhere. I saw the sand coming, so I closed the lid on my wash container with my clothes in it. Mr. (CW3) Price and the other Soldiers who were washing their clothes did not have the chance. All the clothes they just washed got sandblasted. That General was upset because someone stole his bulldozer.

Mr. (CW3) Bingham hotwired the bulldozer a while back. The word I heard, the bulldozer was setting on the Highway for a long time, until Mr. Bingham went and got it to use in our compound. I don't know what type of words the General was telling Major Becker (our Commander) or the outcome. I know there is a guard that is posted to it now.

Later, someone in the First Flight Squad informed me there is a flight tomorrow. I went to the Operation tent and looked on the mission board. I did not see anything on it. Therefore, I walked over to see CPT Babine in his tent, and he just got finished getting the formation altogether for tomorrow's flights. He informed me of the following:
First-up for tomorrow is SGT Red.
Second-up is SSG Mullen.
NVG with SSG Schaberg on AC # 550.
NVG on AC # 735 with SGT Gold.

Day 66: 7 Feb 1991 / Thursday

I got up this morning at 0500 hours (5 am) and woke-up SSG Schaberg. I am supposed to go on a phone run at 0630 hours (6:30 am), and SSG Schaberg will go to Sick Call about his leg. SFC Perez is going to the Staff Meeting at 0630 hours (6:30 am) for me. I woke up with a severe headache this morning.

Well, I am on the back of a 2 ½ ton truck now. SGT Denman is driving, and SSG Schaberg is riding as co-driver in the front seat with SGT Denman because of his sore leg. Inside the truck's back with me is Mr. (CW3) Hunter, Mr. (W01) Gambrel, PFC Bolding, SPC Boettcher, and SPC Cotto. It is freezing riding in the back of this 2 ½ ton truck. It took 1 ½ hour to get to the phone center. When we got there, we did not have to wait very long to use the phones.

I called Cindy, and it was good to talk to her. She said, "I got hired on at Landstuhl General Hospital in the Orthopedic Clinic. My hours are from 0745-1645 hours (7:45 – 4:45 pm), Monday through Friday. Before, there was a hiring freeze with the Federal Government, but the freeze got lifted when the war started."

Cindy said, "Our Ford Tempo was at AAFES (Army and Air Force Exchange Service) Car Garage being repair as the water pump went out. Also, the Battalion is bringing over packages we mail to you all. I sent you a new non-expensive 35 mm camera, as the 110 pocket camera films you sent back did not come out very well." Then she asked about SSG Schaberg. I only got to talk to her for about 10 minutes. It was great talking to Cindy, and I did not want to get off the phone.

We left the AT&T Phone Center and drove to the 818th Battalion area. There we picked up the mail and some packages. I don't know if I got anything or not, but I sure hope I did. I also picked up a few bananas from the Recreation tent and a couple of juices. SPC Cotto gave me one of his MRE. I ate it because I was hungry and had a headache.

When we left there, we stopped by COSCOM (Corps Command) PX. I stayed in the truck to guard the mail and Soldier's equipment. SPC Boettcher brought me a can of pretzels. I gave him $2.00 earlier for it, and he gave me back $1.00. Mr. (CW2) Price got on the truck and said, "I walked up to the PX." Then Mr. Price said, "I received a large package from a private company in the states called 'Wings.' When I opened the box up, the first name badge on the top I pulled up was SSG Hailey." That then reminded me, Cindy had said, "I am sending you the Army Times magazine on SSG Hailey."

When we got back to the Company from the AT&T Phone Run, I dropped off the bag of mail in the Admin tent. Then I walked over and got myself a hot lunch. While I was eating, SSG Mullen handed me five letters. Two from Cindy, one from Penny Suit (oldest step-daughter), one from Joy Suit (youngest step-daughter), and one letter from Jonathan Taylor (my son).

At about 2030 hours (8:30 pm), CPT Babine stopped by the tent and told me, "AC # 726 is still First-up with SGT Kerwin, per SSG Denzel. Also, SSG Niles has, Sergeant of the Guard. The assignment may change tomorrow, as I don't have the Aircraft numbers or Second-up assignment yet." Then he said, "First-up and Second-up helicopters weren't ready today, and they had to get another aircraft."

I'm missing and thinking of my father, Dewey Clarence Taylor, who passed away in Nov 1979 at the young age of 65 years old. He had served in the US Army during World War II. He lost his fingers of his left hand when his machine gun blows up. That did not stop my dad from earning his private pilot license. Even though he was considered a handicap, he never thought of himself as such. And those who knew him did not either. He was the best upholster, father, husband, and friend. I had much respect and love for him, and everyone loves my father.

I wrote Cindy a letter tonight before going to sleep.

Day 67: 8 Feb 1991 / Friday

I slept good last night, nice and warm. I got up this morning at 0500 hours (5 am) and walked over to the restroom. I noticed SGT Walling did an excellent job of blocking the blowing wind from coming into the latrine by putting up plastics over the windows.

SGT Walling put up plastics over the latrine windows; therefore, he did an excellent job blocking the wind from coming in. Photo courtesy of Jim Mullen.

When I got back to my tent, I fixed myself two cups of Mocha, updated my status board, and reviewed my Staff Meeting record book. Then I walked over to the Staff Meeting at 0630 hours (6:30 am). In Company Formation, I informed my Soldiers of the information I received from the meeting.

Later, I saw CPT Connell, and he said, "I am finished now with your EER. I gave you above the best and couple excellence on your report."

I helped SGT Walling to put up some boards in the washing area. Then we put plastic over the top and made a roof. SGT Walling is real created by doing things for the Company. The First Sergeant came by and told me, "We have a Platoon Sergeant Meeting with me at 1600 hours (4 pm)." I informed 1SG, "Monday through Saturday; the flight medics have Medical Training at 1600 hours (4 pm)." First Sergeant replies, "I will fill you in later with the information."

I went to Medical Training at 1600 hours (4 pm) on amputation. SSG Schaberg was a little late coming in for his class he is teaching. It was a real quick class, and I wish he would have given more hands-on training.

After the class, I walked over and got to the tail end of the Platoon Sergeant Meeting. After the meeting, the First Sergeant filled me in on all the information I missed. He said, "Soldiers are not getting the information put out in these meetings." Then he said, "I know you are because I heard you after formation informing your Soldiers." Plus, he talked about the Battalion Command Sergeant Major's visit on Sunday.

Later, I saw CPT Babine, and I informed him what the First Sergeant said about the Soldiers not getting the information put out in the Staff Meeting and his remarks to me. CPT Babine replied, "Good job Sergeant First Class Taylor."

A while later, I saw CPT Babine walking toward me with a smile on his face. He said, "You're going to Dhahran tomorrow on AC # 001". He said, "Be prepared for an overnight stay."

The picture on the left was of Mrs. Tillman when she got married. I was in her 3rd-grade class. I am on her right side, Larry Miller on her left, and is kissing her cheek. The photo on the right is of Mrs. Tillman in her class some years later, in 1991.

This afternoon, I received three letters from Cindy. Also, I received one letter from Mary S. Tillman, my 3rd Grade Teacher. A while back, I looked up her address and wrote to her from out here in the desert. I was surprised to hear back from her, and she wrote a 12-page letter to me. Mrs. Tillman said, "I have been teaching for 30 years, and that is a great Christmas present to receive your letter. That gave me the high spirit to take back to school, knowing I do touch lives." After reading her letter, I answer Mrs. Tillman.

I fixed myself an MRE as I was hungry. Then I read Cindy's letters she wrote on 11 Jan 1991. After that, I went to sleep as I was tired.

Day 68: 9 Feb 1991 / Saturday

I got up this morning at 0500 hours (5 am). I walked over to the helicopter with all my baggage and checked with Crew Chief SSG Woolen on AC # 001. He said, "The flight has changed to after breakfast." I help everyone put their baggage in AC # 001. The two pilots are Mr. (CW2) Dixon and CPT Diane Sanders. Also on board is Maintenance Platoon Leader CPT Dodson and a civilian tech (Airframe & Power Plant Mechanic), Headquarter Platoon Leader CPT Watson, SSG Woolen, and myself.

SSG Sims told me, "While in the breakfast line, I got behind CPT Diane Sanders and attached something to the male end of her aviator protective mask as a joke. I did this while she was not looking". I told SSG Sims, "Sometimes, I don't know about you!"

Well, it is 0823 hours (08:23 am), and we still have not taken off yet to Dhahran. We finally left at 0845 Hours (08:45 am). We made a stop for fuel en-route, and I got some sands and a couple of colorful Rocks from the ground.

We flew into Dhahran and dropped off CPT Watson and the civilian tech. Then we took off and fly to the Port. We waited there while CPT Dodson and Mr. (CW2) Young checked on the new helicopter. While the crew was there checking out the aircraft, I ate an MRE and relaxed a bit.

Photo of Pilot in Charge Aircraft # 001 on our flight to Dhahran Saudi Arabia and Bahrain.

We left the Port at about 1315 hours (1:15 pm) to go to Bahrain. Small Island Country next to Saudi Arabia surrounded by the Persian Gulf. The crew we have now are Mr. (CW2) Dixon, CPT Diane Sanders, SSG Wooten, and myself. We flew into Bahrain to pick up some "Any Service Member" mail from the APO (Army Post Office).

We landed at the airport there, and someone told our crew chief that the APO is a couple of miles away. After waiting at the airport for a while, Mr. (CW2) Dixon gave up on finding the APO and headed back to Dhahran. Bahrain looks pretty nice; I sure wish we could have found the APO there and got to see Bahrain a little more.

We flew into the 45th Medical Company at Dhahran. Once we arrived, I got with SFC Guthro about some Medical Equipment Supply. He gave me the following: 2 MAST Trouser (Military Anti-Shock Shock Trousers – used to treat severe blood loss and maintain blood level), 2 Portable suction machines, 2 KED (Kendrick Extrication Device – uses to immobilizing a patient where you find them), and 2 Body Splints (use to immobilizing the body for possible back/neck injuries). He had me hand receipts for these items. In other words, I had to sign for all this equipment. Then he gave me several 500 ml of Lactated Ringer Intravenous solution (IV solution – used for electrolyte and fluid replacement) and four boxes of 16 gages IV needles.

While in Dhahran at the airfield, I got in this cool jet that read, "Free Kuwait," and someone took my picture.

The crew and crew chief were gone, so SFC Guthro, another Soldier, and I carried the equipment to AC # 001. I walked over to the hanger and asked their maintenance folk to use their Phillips head screwdriver. I took it to the aircraft and took off one screw, and I opened the locked door and loaded the equipment. After that, I returned the screwdriver and told them thanks.

Later, I asked around if anyone knew the location of the Red Cross Office. Someone said, "It is by the PX." I asked the 45th Medical Company 1SG Mankoff, "Which direction is the Red Cross?" He said, "I will get you a ride there." A Sergeant First Class from their Operation gave me a ride to the Red Cross Office.

Once I got there, I asked, "Where is Eric Moe?" They said, "He hasn't been here for a long time. He left here and went with the 24th Infantry Division, and now he is back in the states." I could not believe it. I am here now, I go all the way to Dhahran, and he is back in the states. Well, I completed one of the two missions I set off to achieve for today.

One was to get the Medical Equipment Supply, and the other was to visit Eric Moe, which I did not, as he already left and went back to the states.

I got a ride back to the 45th Medical Company. I did not know where my crew went. I talked with a female maintenance officer captain there. She said, "Your crew took my vehicle and went to the PX."

I talked to SGT Schweyer from the 45th Medical Company for a while. He is planning to get out of service when it comes to his time. Someone there at the 45th Medical Company gave me a Pepsi to drink while we were talking.

Later, I saw our crew by the helicopter getting their baggage. So I ran to the aircraft as the pilots and crew chief was fixing to leave. I got my rucksack out of our Medivac Helicopter and loaded it on the truck. Later, I got off the vehicle with my backpack and got on a bus. From there, we all went to the White Elephant. Their name of the building for the 45th Medical Company.

When I got there, SFC Guthro said, "You can bring all your things to my room and spend the night here." I thought that was nice of him. After that, he and I went and saw a movie down the hall from his room. After the movie, we went downstairs and ate supper. They had fried chicken. It was pretty good too.

SFC Guthro and I talked for a while. He was an instructor at Fort Sam Houston, Texas, back in 1985 –1986. I asked him if he knew a few guys I was a station with during my first tour in Germany and Fort Rucker, Alabama. He knew Roger Brown, Cruz, SFC Cortez Cunningham, and CSM Gibson. SFC Guthro said, "I was in the Marines from about 6 – 7 years. I had a break in service before I joined the US Army."

After that, his friend came in to play Nintendo. So I left to take a bath in a real bathtub. It was great too. When I got finished with my tub bath, SFC Guthro and his friend were gone. So I got in the blue sleeping bag that Cindy loaned me and went to sleep at about 2200 hours (10 pm).

Day 69: 10 Feb 1991 / Sunday

Well, I slept well last night. I got up this morning at 0700 hours (7 am). That is about 9 hours I slept. That is the longest I have slept since I have been in Saudi Arabia. I got up, packed, went, and ate breakfast in the basement. I sat with SSG Wooten, Mr. (CW2) Dixon, and Mr. (CW2) Young. I asked the pilots, "When are you leaving?" They said,

"About 1000 hours (10 am), the bus is going to the airfield." Mr. Dixon said, "If you have anything to do, go ahead, we will depart about 1400 hours (2 pm)."

I went and got two cups of coffee and brought it back up to the room. I gave one to SFC Guthro and kept one for myself. SFC Guthro gave me a ride back to the 45th Medical Company at the airfield. After I got to the 45th Medical Company, I saw CPT Diane Sanders. She asked me, "How you get here?" I informed her, "SFC Guthro gave me a ride." I also asked her the same question. She said, "I got a ride with one of the guys."

Later, the rest of the crew arrived and loaded up their baggage on the helicopter. SFC Guthro said, "You can use my Blazer if you want." So CPT Diane Sanders, Mr. (CW2) Young, SGT Waldron, SSG Woolen rode with me to the PX.

1SG Mankoff gave me $10.00 to get him a carton of cigarettes; SFC Crispin Perez gave me $10.00 for AA batteries before I left camp. I checked at the PX, but they did not have any AA batteries, but they did have cigarettes. So I got 1SG Mankoff his carton of cigarettes. I spent $12.00 of my own money at the PX.

I asked someone there at the Army Post Office if they had "Any Service Member" mail? I was told, "You would have to go to the ASP (Ammunition Supply Point). Then they gave me direction. Once we got there, CPT Diane Sanders asked me to mail her Valentine's Card for her, so I did. I said to someone there, "I came to pick up 'Any Service Member' mail."

They said, "You have to go to ARCENT (Army Central Command / Third Army Command) Chapel Office to get it." Later, SGT Waldron talked to someone there and got many "Any Service Member" mail and packages. I asked him how he did it, and he said, "I told them, I'm the Chapel Assistance." We then drove back to the 45th Medical Company.

1SG Mankoff is the First Sergeant of the 45th Medical Company.

Photo of the 45th Medical Company with their First Sergeant Mankoff upfront.

1SG Mankoff is standing in front of the Desert Dustoff tent of the 45th Medical Company. These three photos courtesy of Jeff Mankoff.

I am thinking of my mother, Margaret Taylor, who is holding my son, Jonathan Taylor, taking in 1985.

Thinking of my brother, Tommy Taylor, as he is holding my son, Jonathan Taylor, taking in 1985.

When I got back to the 45th Medical Company, I used their civilian phone and called Mom. I got to talk to Mom and my brother, Tommy, for about 15 minutes. Tommy wanted me to send him some sand, so I did. Mom said, "I changed your address zip code after watching it on TV about Any

Service Member mail." I informed her, "That is wrong, and to please use the address I gave you. The zip code you saw on TV is for people sending mail to 'Any Service Member.'"

Well, we ended up not leaving today. We all piled up in the back of a pick-up truck and went to the Mission Inn to eat supper. I had fried fish. After we ate, we all went to Saudi PX. There I bought SFC Crispin Perez his AA batteries for $8.00. I have $2.00 to give back to him. I also bought SSG Schaberg, a metal cup-like mine. He now owes me $2.00.

I am thinking of my brother, Tommy Taylor, with my daughters, Penny and Joy, taking in 1985.

Tonight I called out on a TAC (Tactical Air Command) phone from the 45th Medical Company, and I got right through. However, Cindy was not at home. The phone rang for 5 minutes. Then we had to leave, and I caught a bus and rode to the White Elephant. When I got there, I walked up to the TV / VCR room and saw SFC Guthro. I informed him we had not left yet. I asked him, "You still have an empty bed in your room?" He said, "I sure do." So I dragged my baggage to his room and came and watched a movie that they were watching.

After that, we went back to his room. I asked him," Where can I buy a pair of desert boots?" He said, "Try on the pair underneath the cot." I tried it on, and it fits okay. He said, "Those are size 8, and if you like, you can keep those and pay me $40.00". I asked, "Would you take a check, or do you want me to cash a check?" He said, "You could drop it off by finance in the morning. If you don't have a chance, you can pay me later." So I said, "Sure, thanks." Then he started writing a letter. I asked, "Is it alright to take a shower." He said, "Go ahead and take advantage of it while you are here." So I did.

Day 70: 11 Feb 1991 / Monday

Our crew left the White Elephant, 45th Medical Company living quarters at 0745 hours (7:45 am), as that was the time the bus left to go to the airport. On the airfield, I saw all the Free Kuwait Jets departing the airport.

On the sides of these Jets is painted, "Free Kuwait."

We departed with both helicopters at 0940 hours (9:40 am). While flying over the deserts, I saw lots of heard of camels. There were brown, white, and black camels. I have not seen any double hump camels since I been here in Saudi Arabia. CPT Watson is flying back with us in our aircraft, and he has some liquid in his flight bag that is leaking. So he had to clean out his flight bag.

We all got back just in time to eat lunch. I got 2.5 hours of flight time flying from Dhahran. As soon as I walked into our tent, SSG James started whining and asked, "Did you go to the PX?" I told him, "Yes." Then he said, "It would have been nice knowing." I informed him, "It was no secret, and I asked in both tents if anyone needed anything. Also, CPT Diane Sanders came in this tent and asked as well." SSG James said, "I did not know you all were going to Dhahran."

After that, I walked over and got my hot lunch, T-Ration, and took it into the Operation tent to eat. Later, SSG Schaberg got his meal and ate it in the Operation tent too. SSG Schaberg has his Desert uniform on with his regular Green BDU cover over his helmet. It is hard to get a complete set when we are out here in the desert.

We have a nickname for the Desert BDU, we called "Chocolate Chip Uniform," as it reminds us of chocolate chip cookies. SSG Schaberg and I talked for a while, and I informed him what Medical Equipment Sets I pick up while I was in Dhahran. Then Mr. (W01) McCarthy came in and said something smart like, "Clean up your mess after you get through eating."

At 1300 hours (1 pm), our Company taught a class on "Field Sanitation." Rules, such as restrooms, cannot be any closer than 100 feet from any water source.

The Commander wanted to talk with all the NCOs for their help on safety. He said, "My goal when we came here was to bring back 100% of our personnel." Then he said, "I will not be able to achieve that goal, referring to the loss of life of SSG Hailey, but I want to achieve the next one, which is to bring back the rest of the Soldier home."

After that, our Commander answered questions. Someone asked about the mail situation. Our Commander said, "My first letter from my wife took 1 ½ month to get to me." Then our Commander said, "So that it would be handle correctly; I called LTC Love after arriving at the accident scene to inform him of SSG Hailey and the rest of the crew's condition."

This evening, CPT Babine stopped by our tent and gave me the crew lists and aircraft for tomorrow. After he left, I figured out who is Sergeant of the Guard. Then I put out the information to my platoon.

Before I finished fixing myself something to eat, SSG James came whining to me with his endurance sheet. Which are the hours of rest needed for crew members. The first thing I asked him, "Did you see SFC Perez?" He said, "Yes, and he sent me to you." I told him, "Take it to CPT Babine." He continues whining about it, and then SGT Homer started in.

After I finish eating, I took the endurance sheet from SSG James to CPT Babine. While I was talking to him, SSG Denzel came with all of his Soldiers' endurance sheets. CPT Babine and I walked over and spoke with Mr. (CW2) Price, and we talked for a while.

Then I returned SSG Denzel endurance sheets to him. SSG Denzel's group in the first flight squads started asking me questions. I did not have an answer for them. After Company Formation tomorrow, I informed SSG Denzel; I will collect the endurance sheets and turn them to CPT Babine to have the Commander place his signature on them.

Later, I informed SSG Schaberg, "You are flying in place of SSG James, as he is over his endurance hours." Then SSG Schaberg said, "I am over my endurance hours too (required crew rest), and just about everyone is." My thoughts, we need a crew endurance system, but a more realistic one. I went to sleep at 2200 hours (1000 pm). I was exhausted and had a severe headache, plus the movie they had playing in the tent next door did not help my problem any.

Day 71: 12 Feb 1991 / Tuesday

I got up this morning at 0540 hours (5:40 am) and woke up SFC Perez. I told him to get the rest of the Second Flight Squad up for Stand-To at 0600 hours (6 am). Soldiers were slowly coming out of their tents this morning for Stand-To, especially the officers. I sent out seven flight medics, and the officers had three to go to their fighting positions (bunkers).

I went to the Staff Meeting at 0630 hours (6:30 am), but the light went off during the meeting. Our Commander said, "Go get breakfast and come back." So we all went and got our breakfast and brought it back into the Operation tent. In the Staff Meeting, the Commander said the following, "Iraqi has remote control airplane like us that can take pictures. They are wearing protective masks, and they even found NVG goggles in one of their tanks."

Our Commander also said, "We will wash vehicles today so that we can paint upside, 'V,' and 'Red Crosses,' on all vehicles no later than 0900 hours (9 am). The PAO (Public Affair Office) team might be here today to film the unit, and we might be on television in Germany. Also, SGT Holmes should be back in a couple of days from now." Our First Sergeant said, "We will have Church Services at 1300 hours (1 pm) today for both the Protestant and the Catholic faith."

After the Staff Meeting, we had Company Formation at 0730 hours (7:30 am). I informed both First and Second Flight Squads to perform PMCS and wash their vehicles so we can paint the upside-down 'V' and 'Red Crosses' on them before 0900 hours (9 am). Later, I checked our platoon vehicles, and they were all washed and ready to be painted.

Few of the Soldiers before Company Formation. Courtesy of Jim Mullen.

I talked with SFC Perez about his Soldier's needs to start going through him. Also, to let them know, I am not going to put up with Soldiers being disrespectful. SFC Perez said, "I will talk with the Soldiers."

CPT Babine stopped by my tent and told me, "AC # 746 will be Second-up until AC # 550 return back to service." Later, I informed SSG James, "You are Second-up, and SSG Schaberg will be flying with you today. I want to make sure SSG Schaberg is capable of flying again. The reason for this, as you know, SSG Schaberg was in the crash a while back, and it may take a little while until he fully recovers."

When I saw SSG Schaberg, he was in his Desert BDU. I had to tell SSG Schaberg, "You need to get into your flight suit."

When I saw SSG Schaberg, he was in his Desert BDU. I had to tell SSG Schaberg, "You need to get into your flight suit."

SSG Schaberg with his Desert Battle Dress Uniform on and wearing his 38 caliber pistol.

I talked with CPT Babine about putting SSG Clint in the headquarters tent to make room for SGT Holmes. I also suggested putting SSG Davis in the second flight squad tent to make it even between the First and Second Flight Squads. He said, "I want you to look at the rating scheme and get back with me, in case I need to talk with the Commander."

The Dining Facility served a hot lunch today, which is in hot water, and we had to pick the main course, which is in a can. It was not very good.

I washed my clothes today. There are only two washing machines, and the extension cord was missing from one of them. I went to supply and signed for another extension cord. I hooked it up and was washing my clothes. Later, SFC Forest came up storming mad and was fixing to disconnect the extension cord. I said, "I hope you don't plan to take that extension cord because I just signed for it from Supply."

Then he started yelling, so I got up to his face and yelled back. I told him, "Don't go yelling at me." He said, "You can only have one washing machine going on at a time." I reply, "Who said?" He replies, "I said." I reply, "Who in the heck do you think you are?" He just looked at me and said, "Burn out the washing machine; I don't care." After that, he left, and I sat back down and told SGT Walling in a calm voice, "What were we talking about?" He smiles.

After I washed my clothes, I went to Supply and asked for clothespins. CPT Watson said, "How you know about the clothespins?" I reply, "Remember, I helped you load and unload them from the helicopter. Then I helped you unload them from the truck to go into the Supply tent." CPT Watson said, "I want to mark all the clothespins before they go out on the clotheslines." I asked, "Are you going to give me a box of clothespins so I can hang up my clothes?" He replies, "What were you using before?" I said, "Forget it. Just don't ask for my help again."

Later, SSG Miller wanted to wash his clothes. So I started the 5 KW generator for him so that he could do his clothing too. SSG Miller said, "Thank you, SFC Taylor."

I just ate potato chips for supper tonight, as I did not feel like fixing anything. Then I wrote a few letters this evening.

Day 72: 13 Feb 1991 / Wednesday

I got up this morning at 0500 hours (5 am). I woke up SSG Miller, as he wanted me to wake him up when I got up. I went to the Staff Meeting at 0630 hours (6:30 am), and everyone was going to get a hot breakfast. So we all ate our breakfast while we had our meeting.

In the Staff Meeting, they talked about Sunday Church Services at 1300 hours (1 pm), Ash Wednesday at 1830 hours (6:30 pm), and the phone run. I asked, "Any words on SSG Lucia Gabriela?" Mr. (W01) Gambrel said, "Her emergency leave did not start until she arrived in the country, and the same applied when returning."

SGT Penny Suazo went to speak to the Commander about having a party for the unit. She explained to him, "We have been in the desert a long time, and we had been eating MRE's, which can become disgusting very quickly." She went on to say, "A party would boost morale, and we all needed a little boost." The Commander luckily agreed, and she went off to make some plans.

I tried to get SGT Red to sign for the Medical Equipment Set I signed for in Dhahran, but he would not do it. He suggested that I sub-hand receipts (whenever a new person takes over the original hand receipt) as needed. I told him I plan to learn Medical Supply, and I want him to teach me everything I need to know.

I talked with CPT Babine about AC # 700 going into maintenance. He said, "It was going into maintenance, but they got it fixed." Also, I informed him about CPT Watson about the clothespins issues. Then I went out to AC # 550 and did an inventory of all the equipment on board.

Later, SSG James came out to the helicopter. He showed me how he packed his aid bags. He put his bandages all together in one aid bag, and his IV's all together in a separate aid bag that he keeps on the helicopter. While we were talking to each other, they got a First-up mission.

I got with the First Sergeant on the rating scheme and got it corrected. I also informed SSG Davis, he is now in the Second Flight Squad. SSG Davis brought over a cassette tape to our tent that we all listened to, about Saddam Hussein and the Americans.

At about 1400 hours (2 pm), we had a class. SGT Gold gave a lesson on Information Form to use while treating patients in the helicopter en-route to relay to the hospital.

SGT Homer has Sergeant of the Guard tomorrow. SSG Davis wanted to pull it, but SGT Homer wants to pull Sergeant of the Guard. I informed SFC Perez to talk with SSG

Davis. SSG Davis wanted to be up all night to call the states and check on his status of getting selected to flight school. SFC Perez informed SSG Davis he would let him sleep in a litter later the next morning; therefore, SSG Davis is happy. I also talked with SFC Perez on other issues as well.

SSG James informed me, "By the time we landed and got to the auto accident scene, SSG Miller was already treating the patients. SSG Miller was on a phone run and got off the 2 ½ ton truck to help save and treat patients involved in an auto accident."

This evening, we got a box of goodies for the Flight Platoon. SSG Davis brought it over to us in our tent.

Tonight, I wrote a few letters to my relatives, to answer the Christmas Cards they sent me.

Day 73: 14 Feb 1991 / Thursday

Well, today is Valentine's Day. I got up at 0500 hours (5 am). We had Staff Meeting at 0630 hours (6:30 am). The Commander said, "Iraqis are wearing and practicing with MOPP Suit." SFC Forest told our

Commander, "The 5 KW generators by the washing machines won't be running. That every one will have to wash their clothes by hand." Our Commander said, "What?" SFC Forest said, "I had to remove a part off of it and put it on Operation Platoon 5 KW generator for deployment forward." Our Commander asked," How long does it take to remove the part? SFC Forest said, "About 5 minutes." Our Commander said, "The troop needs to be able to wash their clothes, so put the part back on."

We had Company Formation at 0730 hours (7:30 am). At the end of the formation, the First Sergeant asked, "Is there any questions?" SGT Penny Suazo raised her hand and said, "Can I come up front?" Then she said, "We have something for our Commander and our First Sergeant." Then two guys dressed like women came up front next to our Commander and our First Sergeant. SGT Penny Suazo said, "This is your date for the Valentine Party tonight." Our Commander told our First Sergeant, "My date is better looking than yours." It was funny. We all had a good laugh.

Our Commander told the unit, "We will be having a get together this evening, and if you want to contribute to Valentine's party to give cash to SGT Penny Suazo. She will be going to the local town of Hafar Al-Batin to get the rations."

Photo of Finance & Post Exchange at COSCOM in the orange container.

After Company Formation, I walked over to Finance and cashed a check for $50.00. Then I walked to the PX at COSCOM, but they had nothing I wanted. Then I walked back to our compound. My feet were hurting from those new desert boots. The sole is hard and doesn't have any cushion. Also, I think the boot is not my size. I walked into the Operation tent to sign back in.

CPT Babine said, "SFC Taylor, you are just the person I want to see. I have the flight schedule for tomorrow and the next day. I need you to add on the flight medics. The First-up is the same for both days, and so is the Second-up. The reason is, they want to vaccinate us and wanted a different flight medic crew the following day."

I informed my platoon about the Anthrax vaccination shot. Most of the flight medics spoke up and said, we do not want the vaccination shot since it is an experimental drug. SSG Sims flat out said, "I'm not going to take it." SSG James said, "I want to see JAG (Judge Advocate General/military lawyer) if they make it mandatory."

I informed CPT Babine what my Soldiers in my platoon said about the Anthrax vaccination shot. He said, "I will get with the Commander on it."

Later, CPT Babine said, "The Commander was not too happy about the Anthrax vaccination shot either, and is going to check more about it."

Oh yea, at lunchtime today we had a steak lunch. It was delicious too. At about 1230 hours (12:30 pm), we had an unannounced Company Formation. Our Commander said, "There are 3 Scud missiles that are present in the air for a town close by us. He said, "Everyone needs to get their MOPP Gear and stand close to their bunkers."

We have a Scud alert and ordered to go to our bunkers. In photo setting in a chair, SGT Morris, standing up next to him SFC Perez, sitting on top of a bunker with a hat on SSG Schaberg, setting with hands together SSG Marroquin, and sitting in the right corner drinking a Pepsi is SFC Taylor. We were all used to how well the Patriot Missile (Scud Buster) was in intercepting Scuds missile, so we were not worried. Photo courtesy Jim Mullen.

Everyone was sitting, lying on their bunkers, and some even brought their lounge chairs. Others also brought their camera to take pictures. But after waiting a while, nothing happened, so we all disappeared away from our bunkers.

Another view from left to right, SSG Schaberg, SSG Marroquin & SFC Taylor. Photo Courtesy of Jim Mullen.

Later, I heard five Scud missiles, and a few of them hit the nearby town, but no one got hurt, except SGT Penny Suazo. She was in the town shopping on official business when the building she was in began to rumble. That is when the Patriot Missile intercepted the Scud over the town of Hafar Al-Batin. The portions of the Scud hit the building next to the one she was in shopping. She remembers looking at the window next to her, and all the glass was flying toward her.

When she came too, there were Egyptian soldiers by her side pulling the glass from her face, moving debris aside, and getting her up so she could get out of the store and off the streets. There was building destruction throughout the city. The Egyptian soldier helped her find the Civilian Worker she came with to the town. They both loaded SGT Penny Suazo in the car. Then our Civilian Worker and SGT Penny Suazo left Hafar Al-Batin en-route back to our airbase.

We had a Valentine's Party tonight at 1900 hours (7 pm). It turned out pretty well. We had all kinds of good food, such as chickens, pita bread, hot dogs, pizza, chips, candy, alcohol-free beers, and drinks. We all listened to music and had the opportunity to talk with everyone. All the Soldiers and the Civilian Worker had a great time.

Later, I learned that SGT Penny Suazo's head started hurting on the way back to our camp. After she set up everything for the party, she went straight to her cot and went to sleep.

I received a couple of letters today. I received a letter from Laura Johnson (pen-pal from the Any Service Member mail); Laura Johnson is a sweet person. I also received a letter from Mom. She was glad I sent her the government check, as she needed it. She wrote, "You are a wonderful son." It is getting late, so I will close for now.

Day 74: 15 Feb 1991 / Friday

I got up this morning at 0500 hours (5 am). We had Stand-To at 0600 – 0645 hours (6 am – 6:45 am).

Photo of some of my Soldiers standing around our bunkers watching the Jets and Bombers fly overhead.

While we were all standing around our bunkers for Stand-To, we watched the Jets and Bombers head north and return. They were going to Iraq and Kuwait.

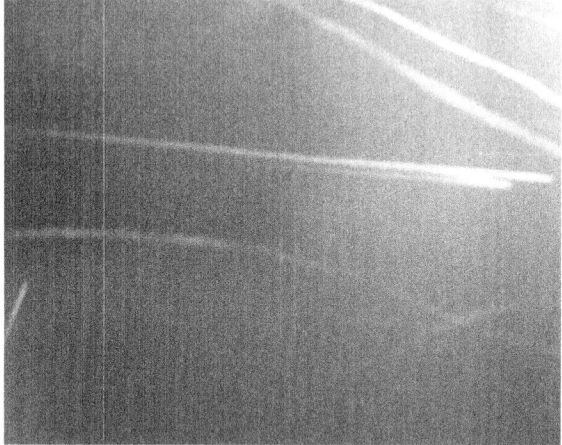

Jets and Bombers are covering the skies this morning.

I took some pictures of the jets flying in the skies.

After Stand-To, we walked over and had a hot breakfast.

Photo of Flight Platoon Sergeant, SFC Taylor during Stand-To this morning while Jets and Bombers flew overhead.

This morning, SSG Schaberg went to sick call to have them check out his injured leg from the helicopter crash a while back. Also, we all had to get the Anthrax vaccine. It was mandatory, and we had no choice.

Today, 1LT Bryant question me about SSG Davis being move from the First Flight Squad to the Second Flight Squad. He was complaining and telling me, "You cannot do this change on my own." I informed 1LT Bryant, "As Platoon Sergeant, I can put them in whatever squad I want too."

Later, I talked with CPT Babine about this. He said, "You did not get back with me about SSG Davis getting a switch from First Flight Squad to Second Flight Squad." I informed CPT Babine, "I thought I did." Then he started questioning me about putting SSG Davis into the Second Flight Squad. I then informed him, "As his Platoon Sergeant, I have that authority." I told CPT Babine, "If you or anyone wants to micromanage me, they can put me in the 45th Medical Company, or I could become a door gunner, or I could become a crew chief on helicopter again. I can even go to the front line; it does not matter." He then questions me no more about this.

I walked over this morning to crank up the 5 KW generator for the washing machines. I noticed the extension cord was missing. I asked SFC Forest, in his platoon formation, if he knew where the extension cord went? SFC Forest said, "I returned it to Supply." I told him, "I am going to get another one from Supply, and you better keep your hands off of it." I asked SSG Diane Riggins, "Did anyone turn in an extension cord to you?" She said, "No."

Later, I talked with the First Sergeant about what he said in Company formation this morning, stating only SSG Clint can run the generators. I informed him, "That was not right for only SSG Clint to run the generators. I went to the class for the generator, and I should be able to run the generators along with the other platoon sergeants that attended the class." The First Sergeant flat out said, "No."

Today, SGT Red gave a class on Field Medical Card. After the course, I went and washed my clothes. I had to get SSG Clint a few times to put water in the washer tanks. SSG Clint asked me, "Will you shut off the generator when you get finished?" I reply, "I sure will."

This evening CPT Babine came up to me acting nice. He said, SSG Davis is in the Second Flight Squad as you planned, and all Squad's Leaders now know. Then I talked to him about the officers not going to Sand-To until late. He said, "For now on when we have Stand-To, we will have a formation at 0600 (6 am). That should take care of that."

This evening, when SSG Schaberg returned from his sick call, the staff giving the Anthrax

Vaccine were already gone. So now he will have to get his Anthrax vaccine tomorrow.

I needed to find someone to pull First-up. I talked with SSG Denzel from the First Flight Squad, and when I asked, he was not very helpful. Later, I spoke with SSG Sims, and he finally said he would pull First-up.

This evening, I wrote a letter. All the letters we write over here are free. Meaning, we do not have to put a postage stamp on them.

Day 75: 16 Feb 1991 / Saturday

I got up this morning at 0545 hours (5:45 am). I walked over and got breakfast. We all ate during the Staff Meeting. There was nothing great put out in the meeting this morning. Our First Sergeant said, "The phone run will be at 1200 hours (noon)." Then I suggested, "Wouldn't it be better to have it after lunch?" Then he said, "Okay, at 1300 hours (1 pm)."

After Company Formation, I put my medical aid bags in AC # 730, and I am pulling Second-up Flight Medic. I am covering for SGT Walling, as he has to get his Anthrax vaccine today. Later, CPT Babine picked AC # 492 for a flight. I talked with SFC Perez; he informed me that SGT Kerwin went as the flight medic on AC # 492.

I stopped by the Supply tent. CPT Watson asked me something about the clothespins on the clotheslines from Supply. I quickly told him, "I have nothing to do with your clothespins."

Then I walked over to my tent and took care of some of my business. Later, Second-up has a mission. So, I grabbed my things and walked over to the helicopter. Mr. (CW2) Clark is the PIC (Pilot in Charge), Mr. (W01) McKenny is the CP (Co-Pilot) Specialist Park is the CE (Crew Chief / Helicopter Mechanic), and myself (Senior Flight Medic / Platoon Sergeant). We flew to Log Base Echo to pick up SSG Lucia Gabriela. Log Base Echo sure is dusty. SSG Lucia Gabriela is returning from emergency leaves. She gave me a hug when she saw me. We also gave someone else a ride back.

When we got back to our camp, SFC Mason said, "I left food out for you guys." After I ate, I walked over to my tent, took a couple of

Tylenol, and laid down as I had a headache. Later, the First Sergeant informed me that Company Formation is at 1000 hours (10 am) tomorrow. He also gave me the times for the Church Services.

At 1530 hours (3:30 pm), I walked over to the Operation tent and checked the mission board. There still were no aircraft numbers written on it. CPT Babine was in there and told SPC Renee Blakey to get the aircraft numbers up on the mission board.

This evening, I recommended to the First Sergeant to give SGT Walling a Coin from our Commander, as he has done an outstanding job working on Field Sanitation for the unit.

Photo of CW2 Elton Clark in front of the Warrants of an Arabian tent.

Day 76: 17 Feb 1991 / Sunday

I got up this morning at about 0800 hours (8 am). CPT Connell came to me this morning and said, "The First Sergeant is out of the net (area) with the Commander. So you are the acting First Sergeant." CPT Connell said, "I need a 2 ½ ton truck, driver, co-driver, and 2 GP Small tents put up." SGT Homer volunteer to be the driver, and SFC Perez volunteer to be the co-driver.

Photo of SFC Inniss, Maintenance Platoon Sergeant.

Later, CPT Connell told me, "It will be 1 GP Medium tent and not 2 GP Small tents." I walked over and spoke with SFC Inniss, the Maintenance Platoon Sergeant, and SFC Forest, the Headquarter Platoon Sergeant. I informed them both I need five Soldiers from their platoon to put the GP Medium tent up. SFC Inniss said, "One of my five Soldiers will supervise putting the tent up." I replied, "I agreed to that."

When I saw CPT Babine, I informed him of the tasks to set up 1 GP Medium tent. Also, the 2 ½ ton truck to pick-up six officers out of battalion, bring them and their baggage here. The GP Medium tent will be their home while they are here with us.

I held the Company Formation at 1000 hours (10 am). I informed the Soldiers of the two tasks' requirements and who had what duties. After that, we had the Staff Meeting. When the meeting was over, I heard CPT Dodson complaining to CPT Connell about his Soldiers having to put up a tent. I walk out as it's not my debate.

I talked with SGT Walling for a little while. We spoke about Real Estate and Nursing careers until the First-up horn went off (meaning the First-up crew has a mission to go on).

SFC Holder came to me and requested a class on Loading and Unloading Helicopters. SSG Mullen said, "I will do it." Therefore, I scheduled the lesson for tomorrow morning at 0900 hours (9 am).

I went to Church Service today. The Chapin Assistance, who is a staff sergeant, is a professional singer. He sang all the songs in the Church Service today. He was supposed to be on the R&R ship, but the U.S. Navy uses the cruise ship for transport instead.

Well, I just got back from Church Service. I received two letters today. One of the letters was from my friend, SFC Cortez Cunningham. We had worked together at Fort Rucker, Alabama, in Plan, Operation, Training, and Security at Lyster Army Hospital. He wrote his letter on 15 Jan 1991. I also received a letter from my sweet Mother. She wrote her letter to me on 19 Jan 1991. What a beautiful, loving Mom, I have.

Day 77: 18 Feb 1991 / Monday

I got up this morning at 0500 hours (5 am) and made myself a hot macho cup. We had Stand-To by our bunkers at 0600 hours (6 am). CPT Diane Sanders was the only officer for Stand-To this morning. CPT Diane Sanders said, "I am going to have to wake-up each officer next time." I informed her, "This is a Failure to Repair," a violation under UCMJ (Uniform Code of Military Justice, for failure to go to the appointed place of duty).

I went to the Staff Meeting this morning. I noticed on the Operation tent's mission board; there were many training flights scheduled for today.

In the morning Company Formation, I informed my platoon of the information put out in the Staff Meeting. I told SFC Perez he is going on Aircraft # 001 as their flight medic. Also, to be at his aircraft by 1000 hours (10 am).

When the Company Formation started, the Commander was looking for SGT Walling. He was not there this morning, as he has Sergeant of the Guard today. I believed the Commander wanted to award SGT Walling the Commander Coin.

At Company Formation, SFC Balch gave a class on NAAK (Nerve Agent Antidote Kit). The NAAK Class is a requirement from our battalion.

Sometime after the morning Company Formation, we started to have many changes or cancellations in the flight assignments. SFC Perez came to me, upset. Mr. (CW3) Hunter gave up SFC Perez Fight

Medic seat to a lieutenant. Now there is no flight medic aboard that helicopter. Later, I heard they received a medevac mission but did not take it because they did not have a flight medic aboard.

We had a hot can lunch for today. It was good, but not great. After lunch, SSG Sims gave a class today on KED (Kendrick Extrication Device) to immobilize a patient where you find them. It was a good class, but I wish he had given more hands-on training.

This evening, I walked over and washed my clothes as it was time to clean again. Later, I got the flight medics assignments for tomorrow for First-up and Second-up. I was able to get Aircraft # 001 from CPT Dodson. Then I informed SSG Davis he has Sergeant of the Guard.

The Aviation Officers put out the Reverse Cycle information (U.S. Army aviation personnel work and sleep hours requirement). The Reverse Cycle does not make any sense to me, and the troops are all complaining about it.

This evening, I walked over to watch a movie the First Sergeant provided. It was called "Major Ledge Baseball." It was pretty funny.

Day 78: 19 Feb 1991 / Tuesday

I got up this morning at 0515 hours (5:15 am). We had Staff Meeting at 0630 hours (6:30 am). Our Intel Reports informed us of the Iraqi conditions. The Iraqi soldiers carry their protective masks but don't have enough MOPP suits (Chemical protective suits). We are also dropping leaflets to the Iraqi troops stating that they are expendable to Saddam and helping them turn against Saddam.

At Company Formation, our Commander awarded SGT Walling a Commander Coin for outstanding work on the Field Sanitation.

After the formation, I walked over and got the helicopter key from SPC Boettcher in Operation to load up the Medical Equipment Sets on the helicopter. I asked SSG Mullen to give me a hand, and he said, "Okay." I walked over and requested SFC Forest for a vehicle, and he quickly said, "No." So I went around him and asked SSG Fox, and he said,

"You can use the pick-up truck when SPC Ward gets back with it in 10 minutes. Also, you will have to get the key for the pick-up from SPC Ward."

Later, I saw SPC Ward heading back to the Motor Pool with the pick-up truck. So I walked into the Motor Pool tent and asked for the pick-up truck. At first, SFC Forest did not want to help me. I told SFC Forest, "SPC Ward can drive; I got to get the medical equipment to the aircraft before they take off." SFC Forest said, "SPC Ward, go ahead."

Once we got the pick-up truck with the medical equipment to the helicopter, SSG Mullen, SFC Perez, and I installed it on AC # 756.

The higher up decided to take AC # 716 instead of AC # 001 for the parts run. I asked SSG Denzel for help earlier but got no one from the First Flight Squad.

This evening, I got the information for all the assigned aircraft and picked a Sergeant of the Guard for tomorrow.

Day 79: 20 Feb 1991 / Wednesday

I got up this morning at 0500 hours (5 am). Today is Mom's birthday, and she is 70 years old. I wanted to call her to wish her a happy birthday, but I had to fly today. After the Staff Meeting this morning, they made changes to the status of the aircraft. They had SGT Kerwin bird as flying. If I got notified sooner when they first made the changes, SGT Kerwin would have pull duty on his bird. I let both CPT Babine and CPT Diane Sanders know my feeling about this.

This afternoon, I went flying north to all the combat hospitals. I flew with CPT Watson PIC, Mr. (CW3) Clark CP, SGT Waldron Crew Chief, and myself (Senior Flight Medic).

When I got back to base camp, CPT Babine came and got me to enter the computer's information in the Operation tent. After we printed the information sheets, I passed them out to my platoon. Then I went back into the Operation tent and used the field phone to call SSG Schaberg at the battalion. He was not there, but I left word for him to call me back. I also informed SFC Perez, in case SSG Schaberg returns the call, he would know what is going on.

This evening, I watched part of a movie called "Hot Dog." After the movie, I went back to my tent. As I was entering the tent, CPT Diane Sanders was leaving. I found out there was another change. I was somewhat upset, but I was glad I got notified ahead of time to make the necessary adjustments.

Later this evening, I talked with SFC Perez. He said, "You're just too nice." I made the necessary adjustment and put SGT Gold on duty for Sergeant of the Guard. SGT Gold and others in the First Flight Squad came up with a plan to do Sergeant of the Guard duties without violating the crew rest requirements.

SFC Perez will cover for SSG Schaberg until he gets back tomorrow.

Day 80: 21 Feb 1991 / Thursday

I got up at 0500 hours (5:00 am). We had Stand-To by our bunkers at 0600 hours (6 am). CPT Diane Sanders had all her officers there this morning. She asked me, "Why you only have four flight medics? She was rubbing it in because on 18 Feb 1991, she was the only officer there, and I said something to her about it. I informed her, "The flight medics that are not here had night duty." She said, "Your night Soldiers were out here before." I said, "They are not going to be here anymore." I asked her, "Are your night officers here?" She said, "No."

I walked over to the Staff Meeting this morning at 0630 hours (6:30 am). Our Commander said, "A General is working on the mail situation in Germany." There was nothing new in the meeting this morning.

After Company formation, I talked with SFC Perez and SSG Lucia Gabriela since they are the squad leaders for our platoon. We talked about several issues.

This afternoon, I walked over and washed my clothes. CPT Rice was at the washing machines. He was my last company commander at Lyster Army Hospital, Fort Rucker, AL. In a meeting a few years ago at Lyster Army Hospital, when my name comes up for an award, he questioned my physical fitness. The company clerk quickly said, "He did max out the last few physical fitness tests and is a graduate of the Army Master Fitness Trainer Course." CPT Rice did not say anything else, per the information I received from the company clerk.

Well, anyway, CPT Rice did not know how to use our washing machines. Therefore, I showed him how to operate it. The washing machines are a lot different than the ones we have back home. After that, we talked about other things. It was good to see him.

Later, I walked over to CPT Rice's tent, he showed me a list of addresses, and I copied the ones I wanted. I wrote SFC Spearman a letter to the 10th MASH (Mobile Army Surgical Hospital) in Saudi Arabia, where he is supposed to be. He and I were stationed together at Fort Rucker, AL.

CPT Connell came to our tent and asked if I needed another flight medic? I never turn down any additional Soldiers I can get. I told him, "Yes, Sir, I will take him." After that, I walked over and talked with the First Sergeant about a GP Small tent, and he went off the handle. I informed him the civilian workers have two tents with two personnel in each. He said, "You want to take one?" I told him, "Yes, I would." Then he went to Supply and demanded to have all the tents hand receipt by today. Well, that never happened.

I looked in SSG Davis tent and figured if they move Standard and Safety, they would have room for two Soldiers in that tent. I informed CPT Babine, and he initiated it. So, SFC Perez, Mr. (CW3) Bingham, Mr. (CW3) Price, and I helped move Standard and Safety into a Small tent that Mr. (CW4) Klase and Mr. (CW3) Price has.

Mr. (CW4) Klase. Courtesy of Bob Klase.

I went to Supply to sign for two cots. Later the new flight medic came. His name is SGT Caito. I was putting the cot together, and one was dirty. I said, "That is what the Supply Officer CPT Watson gave me." I should have seen the Supply Sergeant instead. I don't get along with the Supply officer, ever since the clothespin incident, where he wanted to mark each clothespin before issuing them out. That is the gratitude I got after all the help loading and unloading his Supply a while back.

SGT (SGT/E-5) Holmes and SGT (SGT/E-5) Caito in their tent.

I carried the flight medics' mail to the platoon and gave them out. I got a letter from Mom today with a Valentine Day card, and that was letter number 10 she wrote to me on 21 Jan 1991.

I wrote to Cindy and Mom tonight and then mailed them. It is getting late, so I guess I will go to bed. It is 2300 hours (1100 pm) now, and I am tired. I don't know if the Ground War will start tonight or not.

Day 81: 22 Feb 1991 / Friday

I got up this morning at 0500 hours (5 am). I went to the Staff Meeting at 0630 hours (6:30 am). CPT Dodson said, "Five aircraft are down." Our Commander said, "That is unacceptable. We will talk more about this in private." Our Commander said, "SGT Holmes flew in this morning. The 45th Medical Company flew him here along with packages from Landstuhl and some aircraft parts. The battalion is helping us get personal packages by putting them with equipment and aircraft parts sent to us."

I received a package from Cindy with a new inexpensive 35 mm camera to replace my 110 pocket camera that took poor quality pictures. Also, I received letters from Joy, Penny, Cindy, and the Army Times with SSG Hailey's article. In the package was a Stars & Stripes Newspaper, an extra roll of film and batteries. I answered each one of their letters.

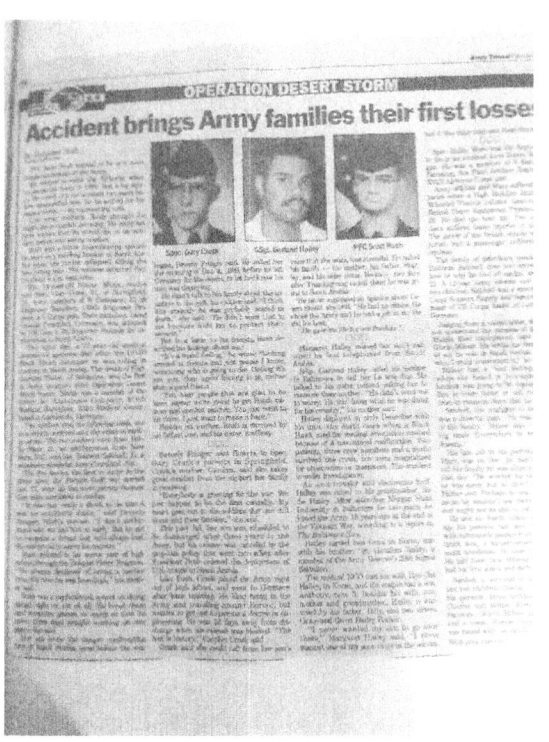

Page from the Army Times with SSG Hailey's article in it.

This evening, I tried to rest some as I had a severe headache. Then CPT Babine came into the tent and got SFC Perez and SSG Lucia Gabriela, and me to go to the Operation tent. In the Operation tent, CPT Babine talked like we should go with the duty roster to solve the problem with Maintenance Platoon not giving the helicopter tail numbers until late in the evening. It looks like CPT Babine sold the ideas to SFC Perez and SSG Lucia Gabriela. I disagreed entirely, but I will try to have an open mind.

Then I walked over to both First and Second Flight Squad tents and explained the duty roster instead of their assigned aircraft. The reason being, we don't get the tail number of the helicopter until late, and CPT Babine feels that will solve the problems. Both squads were upset about these changes. They did not want to get off their assigned helicopter. Some flight medics said they would stop flying altogether. I informed them we are going to have a meeting tomorrow to discuss several matters. Also, to have or not to have assigned aircraft.

Day 82: 23 Feb 1991 / Saturday

I got up this morning late. I got up at 0625 hours (6:25 am). I jumped up and dressed real quick and walked over to the Staff Meeting. In the meeting, was put out the following information: The PX is now closed at COSCOM.

I held a meeting with the flight medics at 1300 hours (1 pm). I told all the flight medics they have a voice, and I will let them decide how to solve it. They all wanted to keep their assigned aircraft.

I talked with Mr. (CW2) Campbell. He said, "You could go with me at 1700 – 1800 hours (5 – 6 pm) to get the helicopter tail numbers for an assignment for tomorrow." SSG Schaberg (Flight Medic) and SGT Zednick (Crew Chief) is on that flight.

Well, anyway, after the class, I walked over to the Operation tent. There was a lot of stuff going on. I said, "SFC Inniss," he replies, "I have what you wanted." He gave me the tail numbers for all the aircrafts assignment for tomorrow, plus the four aircraft flying to the Forward Support. I took that information and figured out who has Sergeant of the Guard. I got SFC Perez and SSG Lucia Gabriela and told them to copy the data and inform their squad.

It was nice to get all this information sooner, so I could relax this evening. Later I walked over and took a shower. When I got back, SSG James offered me some meat that is in a can. So I warmed that up and ate it for my supper.

I noticed someone was playing a VCR movie they received from Landstuhl, Germany, sent to someone's husband. It is playing in the Recreation tent where we have a VCR player. I think it is a home movie someone sent of their family back home. Later, Aircraft # 730 changed from going to 13th Evac to become Second-up for tomorrow.

This evening, Mr. (W01) Rios was in our tent talking Spanish with SFC Perez and trying to act like one of the guys here in our tent. Then SSG Sims disagreed with him about something and said, (curse word) sir. Then Mr. (W01) Rios got in SSG Sims' face and reply, (curse word) sir, don't hit it with me. SSG Sims did not say anything else.

Later, I told SFC Perez, "You need to talk with our Soldiers, tell them these officers come over, and try to act like they are one of us, but be careful they will turn on you." He said, "I agreed with you."

The End

**Platoon Sergeant's Diaries
Book 2, Operation Desert Storm
Persian Gulf War 1990-1991**
-Continue-
**Platoon Sergeant's Diaries
Book 3, Operation Desert Storm
Persian Gulf War 1990-1991**

"Platoon Sergeant's Diaries, Book 3, Operation Desert Storm," is from my second Diary; it starts the day the Ground War began, Iraq Scud Missile hit Israel, Search and Rescued two down pilots. A Flight Surgeon joined our unit to a Claymore Mine found on a POW. A helicopter sitting out in the desert out of fuel and a 38 caliber pistol found in a burn pit. The Iraqi has 72 hours to sign the peace treaty and the burning oil wells, and much more.

Southwest Asia Honor Roll

The following list of soldiers killed in the Persian Gulf area was complete as of March 14.

Of the 176 soldiers killed to that date, 80 died of non-battle causes (22 during Operation Desert Shield and 58 in Operation Desert Storm) and 96 died during combat.

Honoring the fallen.

— Compiled by Heiko Hasenauer

This page is from the May 1991 Soldier Magazine. On the right-hand side is one of our Fallen Hero, "SSG Garland V. Hailey," one of our Flight Medic of the 236th Medical Company, out of Landstuhl, Germany. We honor all our Fallen Hero; they gave it all.

SFC Taylor, Flight Platoon Sergeant, and Senior Flight Medic coming from the Staff Meeting.

The 236th Medical Company wall plaque

I received this plaque upon my departure.

After the war, TDY mission for Vise President Quayle visit to Czechoslovakia. SFC Taylor received a warm welcome in Poprad. This picture is also in the Soldier Magazine, title, Flying Behind the Curtain, November 1991. I also met Ambassador Shirley Temple Black and got her autograph while I was over there.

This picture is the Flight Platoon Sergeant, Sergeant First Class Dewey Taylor, and Platoon Leader, Captain Steve Babine of the 236th Medical Company. Steve found me 25 years plus later on Facebook, and ironically, both of us live close to each other.

Ella & Dewey Wedding Picture, Aug 4, 2000 - Present

Our wedding photo.

In Loving Memories of my Mother,
Margaret Hope Taylor,
Feb 20, 1921 – May 2, 2020

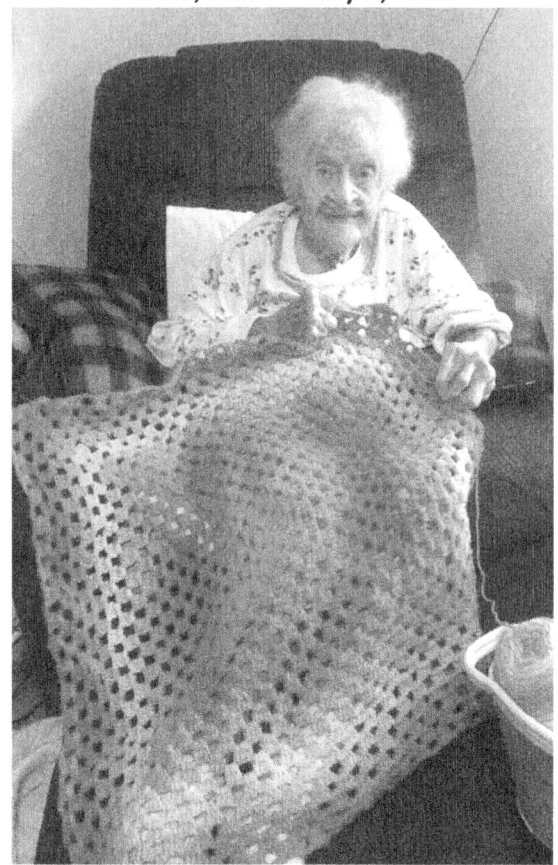

My Mother would knit the most beautiful Afghan and was active on Facebook, email, and message with her iPhone 8+ at 99 years old.

Honoring my Grandfather for his service in the U.S. Army during WW1

My Grandfather, on my Mother's side, Charles H. Hayes Sr. during WW1.

Honoring my Brother for his service in the U.S. Army during the Vietnam Era

Picture from left to right, my sister, Bunny, niece scratching her nose, Scarlet Robbins, and my brother, Thomas Taylor, called Tommy. My brother's graduation picture from Basic Training at Ft. Jackson, South Carolina, in 1972.

For the last several years, I have been a Professional Santa Claus, sharing the Christmas Joy to everyone.
www.SantaJacksonvilleFlorida.com

Final Note

If you found my book interesting, I would appreciate you go to Amazon and write a Review. That would mean a lot to me. Thank you so much.

If you would like to contact the Author, my email address is:
PlatoonSergeantStory@yahoo.com

Thank you again,
Author: SFC Dewey Charles Taylor
Retired U.S. Army

Military Time Conversion Chart

Normal Time	Military Time	Normal Time	Military Time
12:00 AM	0000	12:00 PM	1200
1:00 AM	0100	1:00 PM	1300
2:00 AM	0200	2:00 PM	1400
3:00 AM	0300	3:00 PM	1500
4:00 AM	0400	4:00 PM	1600
5:00 AM	0500	5:00 PM	1700
6:00 AM	0600	6:00 PM	1800
7:00 AM	0700	7:00 PM	1900
8:00 AM	0800	8:00 PM	2000
9:00 AM	0900	9:00 PM	2100
10:00 AM	1000	10:00 PM	2200
11:00 AM	1100	11:00 PM	2300

U.S. Army Rank Structures

Officers are addressed per their rank and Last Name, or Sir/Ma'am.

Warrant Officer

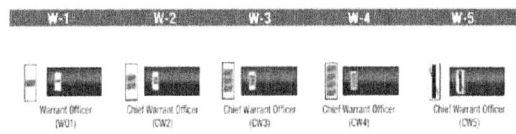

Warrant Officers are addressed per their rank as Mr., Mrs., Ms., or Miss & their Last Name /Sir/Ma'am

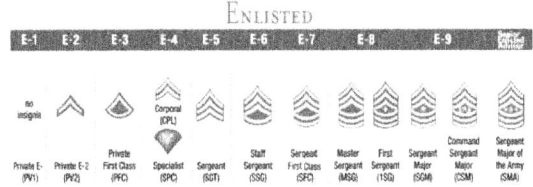

Enlisted are address as follow:

All Privates: Private and Last Name, or just their Last Name.
Specialist: Specialist and Last Name, or just their Last Name.
Corporal: Corporal and Last Name.
SGT E-5 to E-7: Sergeant and Last Name.
Master Sergeant: Master Sergeant and Last Name.
First Sergeant: First Sergeant and Last Name, or "First Sergeant, 1SG or Top."
Sergeant Major: Sergeant Major and Last Name or "Sergeant Major."
Command Sergeant Major: Command Sergeant Major and Last Name or "Sergeant Major."
Sergeant Major of the Army: Sergeant Major of the Army and Last Name.

Abbreviations - Acronyms & Definition

AAFES - Army and Air Force Exchange Service - store.
AAM - Army Achievement Medal.
A Bag - Rucksack (the essential gear [belonging] that will stay with the individual).
AC – Aircraft, helicopter, or bird.
ACOM - Army Commendation Medal.
ACR – Armored Cavalry Regiment.
A&P MECHANIC - Airframe & Power Plant Mechanic.
ADVANCED INDIVIDUAL TRAINING – AIT.
ADVANCE PARTY - Personnel and equipment to set everything up in advance.
AFFEE TRUCK – Food and snack truck.
AFN - Arm Forces Network (television station).
AID BAG - First Aid Bag (with medical supply).
AIT - Advanced Individual Training.
ALL CLEAR - Safe to return to regular activity.
ALSE - Aviation Life-Support Equipment.
AM - Air Medal.
ANCOC - Advance Non-Commission Office Course (Advance Leadership Course).
AO – Is a person sleeping area inside of a tent.
AMNESTY BOX - Box where anyone can turn in illegal items before the inspection begins, such as gun/ammo.
APC- Armor Personnel Carrier.
APO - Army Post Office.
ARCENT - Army Central Command (Third Army Division).
ARMOR KEVLAR FLOORING - Protective flooring from enemy fire.
ARMOR KEVLAR VEST -Bulletproof vest.
ARMOR PERSONNEL CARRIER – APC.
ARTICLE 15 - Military formal punishment.
ASM - Any Service Member (mail from peoples in the USA to show their support).
ASP – Ammunition Supply Point.
AT Ease - A command instructing a subordinate you're out of line and to stop talking.
AUGMENTED – Attached or supplement Soldiers from another unit to increase ours.
B-2 BOMBER – A long-range, massive bombing airplane.
B BAG - Duffle bag / next level of essential gear (belonging).
BACK SLASH / - Minor deficiency.

BDE – Brigade (over several battalions).
BDU - Battle Dress Uniform.
BEANBAG LIGHT SETS - Used to mark landing sites on the ground.
BERM - Dirt wall around the perimeter.
BIRD -Referring to the helicopter or aircraft (AC).
BLACKHAWK - UH-60 Helicopter.
BLACKOUT - All lights turned off to prevent the enemy from seeing from the air or the ground for possible targets.
BN - Battalion (over several companies).
BODY SPLINT - Modified backboard (use to immobilizing the body for possible back/neck injuries).
BULLET STATEMENT – Small statements.
BURNING MANURE - Apx 1/3 of a 55 gal drum used to burn human waste, by putting mogas & lighting it.
BX - Base Exchange (store).
C-12 HARON – Twin turboprop passenger and cargo aircraft / military version of the Beechcraft Super King Air.
C-130 - Transport Airplane.
C Bag - Duffle Bag / with your least important gear (belonging).
CAB - Combat Aviation Brigade.
CAMOUFLAGE POLE & NETS - Cover to conceal.
CAROUSEL - Attach to helicopter interior frame to hold litters for carrying patients.
CAVALIER ARMOR – Bulletproof vest.
CAVALIER FLOOR PLATING – To protect against enemy fire on the helicopter.
CDR – Commander.
CE – Stand for Crew Chief.
CH-54 HELICOPTER - Chinook, twin engines, troop movements & supply helicopter.
CHICKEN ALA KING - A package of MRE.
CHICKEN PLATE - Armor vest (chest plating).
CHOW – Food.
CHOW RUN – Food Run (ride to dinner facility).
CIF - Central Issue Facility.
CIRCLE X - Operational with limitation.
COB - Close of business.
COLOURS - Guidon with Unit Flag.
COMMANDER – Cdr (In this book, referring to our Major/O-4).
COMPANY– Unit.
COMPOUND – Perimeter.
CONEX –Lockable metal storage container.

CONTRACT FOOD - Food prepared & brought to Soldier by outside sources.
CONVOY BRIEFING - Briefing giving before a convoy.
CONUS - Contiguous United States.
COSCOM - Corp Support Command.
COURT MARSHALL - Military punishment under UCMJ.
CP – Co-Pilot.
CRL#2 - Level of Flight Medic Training.
DA FORM 6 - Duty roster - uses to ensure duties are equally distributed.
DA FORM 31 - Leaver request form.
DCU – Desert Combat Uniform.
DD FORM 4186 - Medical Recommendation for Flying Duty.
DEADLINE - Not operational.
DEERS SYSTEM - Computerize lists of an eligible dependent (Defense Enrollment Reporting Systems).
DESERT BDU – Desert Battle Dress Uniform.
DETAIL DUTY – Burning manure.
DIAZEPAM - Valium/treat anxiety, alcohol withdrawal, muscle spasms, or seizures.
DM2 – Demilitarized Zone.
DON MASK - Put on a protective gas mask.
DOS DISK – Disk Operating System.
DUSTOFF - Medevac name.
DUTY ROSTER – (DA Form 6) – is used to ensure Soldiers' duties are fair.
EER - Enlisted Evaluation Report.
EMT - Emergency Medical Treatment.
ENDURANCE SHEET – Hour of rest needed for the crew member.
EPW - Enemy Prisoner War.
ER - Emergency Room.
ETS – Enlisted Time Served (meaning the time scheduled per contract to get out of military service).
FAILURE TO REPAIR - Failure to go to the appointed place of duty under UCMJ.
FALL OUT - A term uses to leave the formation.
FIELD PHONE - US Army TA - 312 Field Phone.
FIELD SANITATION - Rules such as restroom cannot be any closer than 100' from any water source.
FIRST-UP - Crew & Aircraft ready for Medevac mission with little notice.
FLAG ORDER – Fragmentary order (Change in mission).
FLAK VEST - Kevlar Armor Vest.

FIGHTING POSITION – Bunker.
FLIGHT BAG - Bag that carries the flight helmet, flight gloves, and other small items.
FLIGHT PLATOON – Example: 1st & 2nd Flight Squads under one Flight Platoon.
FLOCK– An appointed interim position of leadership.
FORMATION - Assembly of Soldiers lines up in groups by platoons and squads.
FRONT AND CENTER - Military command - 1 step backward, then Soldier report in front of the Commander, salute and say, "Report as directed."
FUEL IMMERSION HEATER – Heat the water going into the shower.
GAM GLOBAL IMMUNIZATION - Global Acute Malnutrition Vaccines.
GATHERING - An informal get together to put out information.
GEAR - Personal belonging.
GI - General Issue – what they call Soldiers.
GP – General Purpose.
GPS – Global Position System (give coordinated with earth latitude and longitude).
GROUND GUIDES - Soldier outside of vehicle who guide the driver back or move within the motor pool.
GROUNDED – Not able to fly for a mechanical reason.
HANGER QUEEN – Helicopter always broken down for one reason or another.
HOT FUEL - Refueled with helicopter engine running.
IC CORD – (Intercom Cord) Attach to flight helmet to helicopter for communication.
ICE PACK - Chemical protective suit.
ID – Identification.
ID CARD - Military identification card.
ID TAGS - Identification Tags, common name, "Dog Tags."
IG - Immune Globulin or Gamma Globulin - to prevent or treat Hepatitis A.
KED - Kendrick Extrication Device –use to immobilizing a patient where you find them.
KEVLAR HELMET - Bulletproof helmet.
KING FAHD INTERNATION AIRPORT - 25 km NW of Dammam Saudi Arabia.
KKMC - King Khalid Military City, or Emerald City at AL Batin, Saudi Arabia.
KP - Kitchen Police/helper, such as peeling potatoes detail.

LAKE CHIEMSEE Resort – Freshwater Lake in Bavaria, Germany.
LAND ROVER - Civilian vehicle the Commander / First Sergeant drove.
LANDSTUHL REGIONAL MEDICAL CENTER - Largest US Army & Department of Defense Hospitals outside the USA.
LATRINE - Field outhouse/restroom.
LBA - Log Base Alpha.
LBE (AREA) - Log Bas Echo.
LBE - Load Bearing Equipment/web belt with two ammo pouches & first aid pouch attached.
LEAVE – Vacation.
LES - Leave Earning Statement – pay statement.
LITTER - Evacuation transport bed.
LOCK AND LOADED – A round of ammo is in the chamber.
LOG BASE ALPHA – LBA (Name of a location, VII Corps located on Tapline Road).
LOM - Legion of Merit.
LOVE BOAT - Passenger Ship at Bahrain, use for R&R that don't leave port.
MAINT - Maintenance/helicopter maintenance and wheel mechanic/keep things working in the field.
MAINTENANCE LOG BOOK – Status of a vehicle or aircraft, such as when service is performed or needed.
MANIFEST - Customs document list of passenger/cargo carried by ship, plane & vehicle to a destination.
MARMITE CAN - Large insulated container used to bring hot food to frontline troops.
MASA – Military Air Staging Area.
MASH –Mobile Army Surgery Hospital.
MAST TROUSERS - Military Anti-Shock Trousers – use to treat severe blood loss & maintain blood level.
MEDCOM - Medical Command.
MED GEAR - Medical Equipment Sets.
MEMORANDUM - Military letter of agreement.
MES – Medical Equipment Set.
MESS HALL-A place where Soldiers go to get their meals.
MESS TENT – A tent used to shelter an eating area.
MI – Military Intelligent.
MPS - Military Postal Service.
MOCHA - Instant coffee with hot chocolate mix.
MOPP SUIT - Chemical protective suit / new set are in what is called an ICE pack.

MOPP LEVEL 0 - Carried: Mask with hood, ready avail; Overgarment, Overboots, & Glove.
MOPP LEVEL 1 - Worn: Overgarment / Carried; Mask with hood, Overboots, & Gloves.
MOPP LEVEL 2 - Worn: Overgarment, Overboots/ Carried; Mask with hood, and Gloves.
MOPP LEVEL 3 - Worn: Overgarment, Overboots, & Mask with hood/ Carried; Gloves.
MOPP LEVEL 4 - Worn: Overgarment, Overboots, Mask with hood & Gloves.
MORALE CALL - Telephone calls (Phone Run) to call loved ones.
MOS – Military Occupation Specialist.
MOTOR POOL - The area where vehicles are kept and maintain.
MOTOR STABLE - Motor pool operation, doing PCMS on vehicles.
MRE - Meal Ready to Eat - prepared food package.
MS - Morphine Sulfate.
MSM - Meritorious Service Medal.
M-2 - Vehicle number.
M9 Paper – Chemical detector paper, used to identify liquid chemical agents present, such as aerosols, nerve, and mustard agents.
M-18 - Vehicle number/ in this case, 2nd Flight Platoon 2 ½ ton truck.
NAAK - Nerve Agent Antidote Kit.
NBC - Nuclear, Biological, and Chemical.
NCO - Non-Commission Officer/ Enlisted rank E-5 to E-9.
NCOIC – Non-Commission Officer in Charge.
NEUTRAL ZONE - Previously shown as diamond-shaped on the map. No military in or near the area.
NET - In the area.
NOMAX - Flight suit – fireproof.
NO SALUTE ZONE – In times of war, saluting is prohibiting in certain zones.
NVG - Night Vision Goggle/ instrument attach to flight helmet for seeing an object in complete darkness.
OER – Officer Evaluation Report.
OH-58D HELICOPTER - Kiowa Warrior Armed Reconnaissance Helicopter.
OPSEC - Operation Security.
OVM – (On Vehicle Material) Are tools, shovel, and other equipment must have with the vehicle to dispatch.
OV-1 Mohawk - Armed military observation and attack airplane.
PA – Physician Assistance.

PAD - Patient Administration, such as the one at the 12th Evac Hospital.
PAO - Public Affair Office – Media film crew, provide a source of information.
PART LOAD LIST - PLL.
PATRIOT - Phased Array Tracking Radar to Intercept on Target, scud buster.
PB TABLET - Pyridostigmine Bromide, anti-nerve agent pill.
PCS – Permeant Change of Station.
PERSONAL GEAR - Personal belonging.
PIC - Pilot in Charge.
PIVOT TUBE COVER – Cover that protects the Pivot Tube.
PIVOT TUBE – A tube attached to the outside front of an aircraft that receive force air to an indicator that reads airspeed in knots.
PLL - Part Load List.
PMCS - Preventive Maintenance Check Service/ an inspection performed before dispatching a vehicle.
POL - Petroleum, Oil, and Lubricants.
POLICE CALL - To form a line arm length apart for picking up trash.
PONCHO W/LINER - Military raincoat with a liner to keep warm/ use for multiple purposes.
POW – Prisoner of War.
PT - Physical Training.
PX – (Post Exchange) Is a place to shop for goods.
QUARTERS (MEDICAL) - Military medical terms for bed rest.
QUARTERS - Military term for Government Housing.
RANGER SLEEPING BAG - Made from a poncho w/liner.
REAR SUPPORT – Support back at home base for us here in the desert and our spouses.
RED DRAGON - Iraq Scud Alert. Everyone into the bunker in MOPP Level 1, wait for instruction.
REVERSE CYCLE - US Army Aviation Personnel work and sleep hour's requirements.
RED X – Ground an aircraft where it cannot fly or a vehicle where it cannot drive.
REPORT OF SURVEY – An investigating report against the person signed for lost, damaged, or missing equipment.
RIYAL - Saudi Arabian Riyal / SAR – Saudi Arabian money.
R&R - Rest and Recuperation.
RTO – (Radio Telephone Operator) Is a heavy radio that is carry on the back of an individual.
RUCKSACK - Military backpack.
S-1 - Military Personnel Office.

S-2 – Military Intelligence.
S-4 – Logistics.
SABOTAGE - To weaken another entity.
SAT PROGRAM - Stanford Achievement Test / to measure knowledge of elementary school for students.
SCATTER PLAN – Evacuation Plan.
SECOND-UP - Crew & Aircraft, become 1st UP when 1st UP gets activated.
SET UP – Frame.
SFQC – Special Forces Qualification Course.
SHAKEDOWN INSPECTION - looking for anything illegal.
SICK CALL - Military personnel requiring medical attention.
SLASH / - In logbook to note minor deficiency.
SQT – Skill Qualification Training.
STAFF MEETING –Commander and First Sergeant Meeting with Platoon Leaders & Platoon Sergeants.
STAIRWELL QUARTER – Military Housing.
STAND-DOWN - Cessation of offensive actions & prepare to go home.
STAND-TO - Short for "Stand to Arms."
STATEMENT OF CHARGES – One must be reissue items and charge for the thing missing.
SUB-HAND RECEIPT - When a new person takes over an original hand-receipt.
SYRIA - Country in the Middle East that is friendly with the USA.
TAC – Tactical Air Command.
TDY – Temporary Duty.
TOC -Tactical Operation Center.
TOE - Table of Organization Equipment.
TOP OFF - Full of fuel.
TPL - Thermos Plastic Liner – in flight helmets.
TURRET – M1A1 Abrams Tank, the part with the big 12 mm gun set on the tank that rotates.
UCMJ - Uniform Code Military Justice – Military legal code and regulations.
UNIT – Company.
VISOR - Nickname for the NVG Goggle.
VENT - Open up and talk about what is on your mind.
VISORS – Hook up to the flight helmet that the NVG is attached.
WAR BOOTY - War Trophy, souvenir items collect from war.
WARRANT OF ARABIA - Warrant Officer Tent – they name it.
WATER BUFFALO - Water trailer with a tank of clean potable drinking water.

WHITE ELEPHANT – The 45TH Med Company living quarter in Dhahran, Saudi Arabia.
WASH RACK – Place for washing military vehicle and aircraft.
WAR TROPHIES - Souvenir of war.

Printed in Great Britain
by Amazon